I'M NOT ALONE

A Teen's Guide to Living With a Parent Who Has a Mental Illness or History of Trauma

Updated and Expanded Second Edition

Michelle D. Sherman, PhD ABPP

DeAnne M. Sherman

Seeds *of* Hope Books™

I'M NOT ALONE: A TEEN'S GUIDE TO LIVING WITH A PARENT WHO HAS A MENTAL ILLNESS OR HISTORY OF TRAUMA
© copyright 2024 by Michelle D. Sherman and DeAnne M. Sherman. All rights reserved. No part of this book may be reproduced in any form whatsoever, by broadcast or transmission, by translation into any kind of language, nor by recording electronically or otherwise, without permission in writing from the author, except by a reviewer, who may quote brief passages in critical articles or reviews.

ISBN Paperback: 979-8-9910362-0-7
ISBN ebook: 979-8-9910362-1-4

Library of Congress Control Number: 2024922084

Book design and typesetting: JamesMonroeDesign.com

Printed in the United States of America

Second Edition: October 2024
First Printing: July 2006
29 28 27 26 25 24   6 5 4 3 2 1

 St. Paul, MN
Visit SeedsOfHopeBooks.com

PRAISE FOR THE FIRST EDITION OF *I'M NOT ALONE*

An informative, remarkably sensitive book that provides youth with the information and compassionate support that will make their difficult journey easier. It is essential that this book be made available to teens dealing with mental illness in the family. It could make all the difference in the world.

—**Fred Sautter, PhD**, Tulane University

A calming, outstretched hand in the middle of an emotional storm…it offers hope to teens who may feel that they are walking a tightrope and their lives are out of control. A tremendous gift for every parent who lives with a mental illness to give to their teenage children.

—**Marcia Hayes**, Past Executive Director,
Depression and Bipolar Support Alliance (DBSA) Oklahoma

A "must-have" book for school counselors, clinical child psychologists, child and adolescent psychiatrists, clinical social workers, and all other mental health professionals working with families…a "must-read" book for youth who have experienced a parent's schizophrenia, depression, or bipolar disorder. No-nonsense yet compassionate, practical yet deep, and concise yet thorough, it provides information, emotional support, coping resources, and a hands-on approach to problem solving for those millions of youth whose parents display troubling, mysterious, and anxiety (and guilt) provoking psychological disturbances. Highly recommended.

—**Stephen P. Hinshaw, PhD,** University of California Berkeley;
Author, *Another Kind of Madness: A Journey through the Stigma and Hope of Mental Illness*

A terrific book. It is clear and to the point…respectful but challenging. It creates a partnership with its readers.

—**Lisa B. Dixon, MD, MPH,** Columbia University Medical Center

Reading its pages is like having a heart-to-heart conversation with an empathic, knowledgeable mentor or an insightful, wise clinician.

—**Teresa L. Arata-Maiers, PsyD,** Brooke Army Medical Center

Excellent resource—practical yet sensitively written. Clinicians working with persons with serious psychiatric illnesses and their families will find this an invaluable addition to their libraries and their clinical work.

—**Shirley M. Glynn, PhD,** University of California, Los Angeles

What an amazing resource for young people, families, and professionals! It should be on the shelf of every mental health professional who works with families.

—**Teresa Peden, MPH, MAMFT,** Former Executive Director, National Alliance on Mental Illness (NAMI), Oklahoma

A reader-friendly text that helps adolescents understand what is happening to their parents, and more importantly, gives them HOPE and strategies to understand their own complicated feelings.

—**Kira Armstrong, PhD, ABPP-CN,** Formerly with Harvard Medical School

Answers teens' questions about mental illness and imparts hope and understanding of their parent's problems. A truly inspired self-help guide.

—**Carolyn Archer**, Certified Recovery Support Specialist

Authors very obviously know the teen mind - soothing, reassuring, and factual. Comforting and enabling: Yes, your parent is ill. No, you didn't make it happen. Yes, it could happen to anyone. Yes, you can still have a life. It takes the mystery out of strong emotions.

—**Jeanette Pelton, LISW-S,** *The New Social Worker Online*

Thorough, supporting, engaging, and right on target for teens.

—**Nancy Petree,** NAMI Family to Family teacher

Guide? Resource? Tool? Interactive journal? All four terms describe Sherman & Sherman's practical books. Provide teens with a blend of developmentally appropriate information and blame-free support with a personalized resource as they learn to cope with trauma and mental illness in their world.

—**Jessica T. Amorosa, EdS**, *Connecticut School Psychologist*

TABLE OF CONTENTS

PART FOUR: Taking Care of Your Own Mental Health

WELCOME

If you have this book in your hand, you are probably experiencing some challenging times with one of your parents. Maybe your mom is depressed, and you are **sad** or **frustrated** to see her hurting. Maybe your stepdad has mood swings and seems happy one day but angry and out of control the next—how **confusing**. Perhaps you feel **embarrassed** when your dad shows up drunk at your basketball game. You may **worry** what will happen if your mother is re-admitted to the hospital and fear she might lose her job. Perhaps you feel **hopeless** and wonder if things will ever get better. Maybe you feel **lonely** because no one understands what you're going through. Perhaps you are **afraid** that one day you might develop an illness like your parent. On top of all this, you might be really **angry,** asking yourself, "What is going on and why is it happening?"

These feelings and questions are very common.
You are not alone.

In this book you can learn about:

✓ Causes, symptoms, and treatments of mental illness/posttraumatic stress disorder (PTSD)…and the very real possibility of recovery

✓ Healthy coping skills

✓ Tools for talking with your friends

✓ How to identify people who can support you

✓ Strategies to strengthen your relationship with your parent

✓ Steps you can take to strengthen your own mental health and resilience

A few points as we begin:

Use this book however you wish. See what sections apply to your situation and skip whatever doesn't feel relevant. There's no need to read the chapters in order.

How about you?

Reflection questions are sprinkled throughout the book. There are no right or wrong answers. If you feel like writing a few words or phrases, go for it. If not, that's OK, too. Please don't worry about spelling, grammar, or complete sentences. Don't try too hard to get all your thoughts and feelings down perfectly—just start writing and see what happens. Literally putting pen to paper can help you process and understand your experiences in a new way. Interestingly, research has found that writing about deeply personal thoughts and feelings can produce many benefits, such as improved sleep and decreased depression and anxiety. You may find the list of feelings at the end of the book to be helpful as you write.

Be thoughtful about where you keep this book. It is important that you feel comfortable writing without worry that someone might read it. If you prefer, or if this book is not your personal copy, you could record your responses in a private journal/notebook or in digital form.

In sorting through your feelings, you may choose to open up to a trusted family member, friend, teacher, or counselor. You could use this book to help start a conversation about what you're experiencing. Whatever you decide, it's up to you.

Reading this book may spark additional questions. The Resource List on page 133 describes organizations and books where you can learn more. The chapters that follow may stir up some challenging, uncomfortable emotions. It takes courage to look inside yourself and face difficult things that may seem easier to ignore. However, dealing directly with your feelings can help you cope better, both now and in the future. Please remember that emotions are not right or wrong. They just are…and they can provide you with information and help you learn about yourself. This book describes many ways to cope with strong emotions, and a list of activities to help get through tough times is on page 131.

Finally, for ease of reading, the term "parent" is used throughout the book. However, that word can refer to anyone who is involved in caring for you, including a birth parent, stepparent, grandparent, adoptive parent, foster parent, or any other guardian.

We hope this book provides you with helpful information, reassurance that you're not alone, strategies for managing difficult situations, and tools for taking good care of yourself.

Michelle and DeAnne

PART ONE

Getting Started

CHAPTER 1

Just the Facts

To set the stage for the rest of this book, this chapter presents eight key facts about mental illness and trauma. Each of these will be explored in detail in the chapters that follow. Let's take a look at these important concepts:

 **FACT #1:** *Mental illness is a real medical condition that involves difficulties with feelings, thoughts, and behavior.*

A mental health disorder is more than just having a bad day or experiencing passing anxiety. With mental illness, the set of symptoms must last for a while (the specific duration depends on the diagnosis) and:

- Be upsetting—often causing extreme worry or sadness

  or

- Make it hard to participate in everyday life such as work, school, or relationships

In addition, the symptoms cannot be caused by alcohol or drugs, prescribed medications, or another medical condition. Just like with physical health problems, a mental health diagnosis should be made by a trained professional.

About 20% of adults experience a mental illness each year.

Mental illnesses are among the most common health problems—far more common than cancer, diabetes, and heart disease. In fact, about 20% of adults worldwide experience a mental illness *each year*. Further, over half of all people will have a mental illness *at some point in their lifetime.*

Serious mental illness (major depression, bipolar disorder, and schizophrenia) is a specific subset of disorders that affects about 1 in 20 adults. **No matter what illness your parent is managing, you are definitely not alone.**

FACT #2: *Mental illness can have many different causes.* Stressful life experiences, trauma, and heredity can all contribute to someone's risk of developing emotional problems. Mental illness may be triggered by difficult situations such as poverty, death of a loved one, racial discrimination, and many other factors. Later chapters address these complex issues in more detail, but please know: **You did not cause your parent's illness.**

FACT #3: *Each person's experience of mental illness is unique.* Although depression, bipolar disorder, and schizophrenia typically emerge during the late teens or 20s, problems can develop at any time. Symptoms may appear suddenly or surface gradually.

The course of mental illness can vary greatly. For instance, two people with major depression may have quite different journeys. Let's consider Terry and Franklin:

Terry is a nurse at a primary care clinic, and lives with his partner and two teenage daughters. He has been depressed for as long as he can remember, but lately things have gotten a lot worse. He has no interest in family activities, and his irritability makes him hard to live with.

Terry takes a leave of absence from work and attends an intensive outpatient therapy program. He learns skills that will hopefully help him to feel better, reconnect with his family, and return to work. His boss and family are worried about him, and they are doing whatever they can to be flexible and supportive.

No one would guess that Franklin is in a deep depression. On the outside, his life looks perfect. He is a highly respected attorney, his social media posts show amazing family vacations, and he enjoys weekly racquetball games with friends.

Inside, however, Franklin is hurting deeply– and it's worse because no one knows. He drinks heavily at night,* fears his wife is going to leave him, and worries he's going to lose his job because he's just not keeping up. His sadness feels unbearable, and he's afraid of telling anyone what's really going on inside.

*Note: Some people managing a mental illness drink alcohol excessively or use drugs to cope with emotional pain; however, these behaviors often create more problems in the long run. Chapter 7 explores the complicated relationship between mental illness and substance abuse.

As you can see from Terry and Franklin, just knowing that someone has depression may not tell you a lot about their unique experience. **The same illness can look quite different from one person to another.**

FACT #4: *Although many people experience a traumatic event at some point in their lives, the vast majority do not develop long-term difficulties.* Chapter 5 explains who may be at higher risk for having lasting problems (risk factors). Chapter 6 describes posttraumatic stress disorder (PTSD), a condition that affects approximately 6% of people at some point in their lives. **It's common for teens to have both empathy for their parent having experienced trauma as well as frustration with their confusing, hurtful behavior.**

FACT #5: *Many effective treatments exist for mental illness, and recovery is possible.* New therapies and medications are continually being developed (see Chapter 8 for more details). Even if your parent is currently struggling, there's good reason to be hopeful that they can continue on their journey of recovery—enabling them to have close relationships, well-managed symptoms, and a life with meaning and purpose. **Hold onto hope.**

FACT #6: *Mental illness affects the entire family. It's important for everyone to take good care of themselves.* Loving someone with mental health problems can be hard. You, your siblings, your grandparents, and your other parent may experience a wide range of feelings and reactions. Just as your parent's mental health can be unpredictable and change over time, your journey can have ups and downs as well. **Having your own support system, enjoyable activities, and dedicated time for your own well-being are important.**

FACT #7: *Teenagers can support their parent in many ways, but it's important to have boundaries. Teens can work to balance helping their parent with living their own best life (which may be easier said than done).* You can express your love for your parent in many ways—spending time together, helping around the house, or sending funny text messages. Sometimes just going for a drive, watching a movie, or playing cards together can be enjoyable. However, try to strike a balance between supporting your parent and paying attention to your own well-being. **You are not responsible for your parent's happiness.**

FACT #8: *There's a lot you can do to strengthen your own mental health.* Throughout the book we offer many tips for taking care of your own well-being and building resilience (Chapter 16 summarizes these recommendations). It's helpful to focus on what you can control, learn about mental illness and warning signs, seek help early, and make healthy lifestyle choices—being physically active, getting enough sleep, eating a healthy diet, and being careful about your use of substances. **Although you cannot change your genes, your family, or your past life experiences, you have a lot of control over how you cope with difficulties and care for your physical and mental health.**

Mental Health Matters

Given these facts, it's clear that mental health is a key part of overall well-being. It affects and is affected by all the other kinds of health—physical, financial, spiritual, environmental, and social. Many aspects of health have two-way relationships. For example, depression can have negative impacts on close relationships—and problems in relationships can lead to depression.

All areas of health fluctuate over time. Physically, we can go through periods of good health and then experience both passing problems (e.g., the flu) and chronic conditions that require long-term management (e.g., diabetes). Mental health is no different. Problems with our thinking, emotions, and behavior can ebb and flow over time, and they can range from mild to serious.

When mental health symptoms arise, sometimes we manage them by drawing upon good coping tools and supportive people, and the problems diminish or disappear altogether. However, other times symptoms persist, become intense and overwhelming, and interfere with everyday activities and relationships. A mental illness is diagnosed when a person experiences a specific set of symptoms. There are over 250 distinct mental illnesses, and people can experience more than one at a time.

When thinking about symptoms of mental illness, it's essential to consider the role of culture, which can include ethnicity, generation, social class, nationality, religion/spirituality, and geography. Every cultural group has distinct norms, beliefs, values, rituals, and language. For example, the military is a specific culture marked by long-standing traditions, strong respect for authority, rules for clothing and grooming, commitment to duty and sacrifice, and strong camaraderie among members. When thinking about mental health concerns among military personnel, it's important to consider messages they may

have heard about self-sufficiency, stigma surrounding mental illness, and the potential impacts of seeking help on their career.

The treatment process must also be responsive to culture. Who people confide in, their preferred coping strategies, and the treatment approach(es) they desire can vary greatly across different groups. For example, people from some ethnic groups experience emotional distress largely in their bodies such as headaches, stomachaches, and body aches. They may experience shame and considerable stigma surrounding mental illness and asking for help. Also, they may prefer or want to incorporate traditional healing approaches with more formal Western mental health services.

Thus, the diagnosis of a mental illness requires much more than just reading a list of symptoms on the internet. Healthcare professionals need to consider an individual's culture and other aspects of their health when making a diagnosis and offering treatment recommendations.

Organization of This Book

This book is organized in four sections. In **Part One,** we preview key facts that are addressed throughout the book. You also have the opportunity to complete a self-assessment of how things are going with your family.

Part Two, the most information-heavy section of the book, focuses on four specific mental illnesses, including:

- **Major depression, bipolar disorder, and schizophrenia** (Chapters 3–4): These are often termed "serious mental illnesses" as they can significantly interfere with one's ability to carry out major life activities such as school or work, healthy relationships, and self-care activities.

- **Posttraumatic stress disorder or PTSD** (Chapters 5–6): This is sometimes classified as a serious mental illness, but it has several clear differences, especially regarding cause.

The rest of the book addresses parental mental illness broadly, without focusing on any specific disorder.

Part Three guides you in exploring your feelings and describes research-based skills for coping with them. You will learn about stigma and discrimination around mental illness, and think through what to share with your friends. We will offer tips for coping with several crisis situations, such as hospitalization or suicidal behavior. Finally, we'll review ways to strengthen your relationship with your parent.

Finally, **Part Four** helps you consider how to manage your own risk for developing a mental illness. We will review specific strategies to build your resilience, including focusing on what you can control. You will also have the opportunity to reflect on what you have learned about yourself and your family.

CHAPTER 2
Snapshot of Your Story

We encourage you to take a few minutes to complete this self-assessment. These questions can create a snapshot of how things are going for you and your family and will set the stage for the chapters that follow.

You and Your Family

Who do you live with? _____

_____

What do you like to do when you are not at school?_____

_____

What do you enjoy doing with your family?_____

_____

Every family has difficulties. What are the biggest sources of stress for your family right now? _____

_____

Who do you feel most supported by in your family? _____

_____

What is your overall stress level?

1	2	3	4	5	6	7	8	9	10
Very Low				Moderate				Very High	

How much is your family aware of how you're doing emotionally?

1	2	3	4	5	6	7	8	9	10
Very Little				Somewhat				Quite a Bit	

How about you?

Your Parent's Mental Health

How about you?

How much do you understand your parent's mental health problems?

1	2	3	4	5	6	7	8	9	10

Very Little   Somewhat   A Lot

How openly does your family discuss your parent's mental health?

1	2	3	4	5	6	7	8	9	10

Very Little   Somewhat   A Lot

How has your parent been feeling emotionally over the past couple months?

1	2	3	4	5	6	7	8	9	10

Poorly   Ok   Very Well

Has your parent been diagnosed with a specific mental illness that you know of? If so, write it here: _____

_____

When your parent is struggling emotionally, what do you notice? Describe specific behaviors (such as sleeping a lot, being jumpy and tense, talking in a confusing way, getting angry over little things, isolating, or crying frequently):

_____

_____

_____

_____

Thinking Back

Do you remember who first told you about your parent's illness?   Yes   No

- If yes, who told you? _____

- How did you feel at the time? _____

  _____

- What did you wonder or worry about? _____

  _____

How old were you when your parent started having mental health problems?

- ❏ Before I was born
- ❏ 0-5
- ❏ 6-12
- ❏ 13-18
- ❏ 19 or older
- ❏ I don't know

[If you remember your parent before they struggled with their mental illness]:
How has your parent changed since developing the illness?

- Now they (or they no longer):_____

  _____

- I miss: _____

  _____

How about you?

Current Worries

How about you?

What are your biggest concerns or worries about your parent right now?

_____

_____

Do you worry how your parent's illness affects others in your family? If so, describe: _____

_____

What is the hardest thing for you about your mom/dad's mental illness?

_____

_____

Pride and Hope for the Future

How about you?

What do you admire about your parent? _____

_____

Does someone step in to help your parent/family during tough times? If so, who perhaps grandparent, aunt/uncle, neighbors, or friends? What do they do?

_____

_____

What gives you hope about your parent's well-being? _____

_____

Perhaps your answers to these questions are part of your motivation for reading this book. We hope that the information and activities in the chapters ahead will help you cope with your parent's mental illness and strengthen your own emotional well-being.

PART TWO

Understanding the Basics

Mental Illness

Trauma

Other Important Topics

CHAPTER 3

Common Symptoms of Mental Illness

There are many different types of mental illness. For example, people may struggle with overwhelming anxiety or depression, issues related to eating and body image, problems with attention or focus, difficulties with alcohol or drugs, or painful reactions to trauma.

The symptoms of mental illness typically involve difficulties with feelings, behavior, and thoughts:

■ **Feelings**
Some people become overwhelmed by intense emotions, while others struggle to understand and experience feelings at all—their own and those of other people. Emotions are what connect us to each other, so difficulties in this area often affect relationships.

■ **Behavior**
People's behavior may change when experiencing a mental illness, such as stopping activities they used to enjoy, having angry outbursts, withdrawing from others, or engaging in extreme or risky behavior.

■ **Thoughts**
Thought patterns and speech can also be affected. For example, people may talk quite slowly or quickly, and may jump from one topic to another. They may say things that are illogical and hold unusual beliefs, such as thinking they have special powers or are a famous person. Others develop negative thoughts about themselves or worry that people are out to get them.

Each mental illness has specific symptoms that can affect overall well-being, daily routines, and relationships. Remember from Fact #3 that the experience of these illnesses can be quite different from one person to another. For example, one person with depression may have no appetite and sleep a lot, whereas someone else with the same illness may eat more than usual and struggle with insomnia.

Most people begin experiencing symptoms of mental illness in their late teens to mid-20s, but schizophrenia can emerge in the early 30s, especially among women. Over the course of the illness, some people experience long periods of stability; they may go into remission, having very mild or no symptoms at all. Others have a more chronic course with periodic ups and downs, relapses or crises, and so-so periods. Sometimes the reason for the change in well-being is clear, such as the death of a family member or loss of a job; other times there isn't a specific trigger. Although recurring symptoms can be discouraging and challenging, people can learn to cope effectively and have meaningful activities and enjoyable relationships.

Although the information in this book applies to a wide range of conditions, we focus specifically on the following three serious mental illnesses in this chapter:

Major depression

Bipolar disorder

Schizophrenia

Major Depression (Major Depressive Disorder)

People dealing with major depression experience deep sadness and/or lose interest in everyday life. This illness is very common; in fact, 1 in 5 people in the United States experiences it at some point in their lives. Everyone in the family is affected when someone experiences major depression.

Let's meet Kai and see how his depression has ripple effects on his wife and children, especially his daughter, Akira.

Kai is a software engineer at a local start-up business. He and his wife, Naomi, have three children and both parents work hard to support the family. Kai has experienced low-grade depression since his early 20s. He finds his antidepressant medication and support group to be helpful.

Three months ago, Kai lost his job and has been unable to find another position. He has sunk into a deep depression. He spends most of his time scrolling mindlessly on his phone, and he looks so sad. Although he used to love following his favorite college basketball teams, he no longer watches any games. His kids often find him sleeping on the couch in the middle of the afternoon. Lately Kai has wondered if his family would be better off without him.

Akira, age 13, feels confused and lonely. Because of the family's financial problems, her mom is working overtime and is hardly ever home. Akira's older sisters are occupied with their friends and school activities. Everyone is always busy, and no one is talking about her dad. Akira feels heartbroken and scared when he makes comments about suicide.

Although a mental health diagnosis should only be made by a trained professional, it's possible that Kai may be experiencing major depression.

People living with this illness may experience the following symptoms:

- Feel very sad or down

- Feel tired and low on energy much of the time

- Sleep a lot or not able to sleep well

- Lose their appetite or be especially hungry

- Lose interest in fun activities

- Struggle to concentrate and make decisions

- Think about death or suicide

- Feel keyed up and restless or slowed down

Remember that everybody has days when they feel tired or sad. That is normal. Major depression, however, involves having quite a few symptoms for several weeks and having difficulty keeping up with daily routines and responsibilities. Kai's comments about suicide are very frightening for Akira; Chapter 15 addresses strategies to deal with that difficult situation.

How about you?

Do you notice your parent experiencing any signs of major depression? If so, which ones? _____

_____

Which symptoms are toughest for you? _____

_____

How do you feel when your parent is struggling with these problems? The list of feelings on page 130 may be helpful. _____

_____

Throughout this chapter, we list the names of famous people who have been open about their experience of mental illness. It is hoped that their public self-disclosure helps to raise awareness, normalize emotional problems, and decrease stigma surrounding mental illness.

Famous People With Depression

Simone Biles, gymnast

Kid Cudi, rapper

DeMar DeRozan, basketball player

Eminem, rapper

Billie Eilish, musician

Lady Gaga, musician

Billy Joel, musician

Elton John, musician

Dwayne "The Rock" Johnson, actor

Mark Twain, writer

Lizzo, musician

Kevin Love, basketball player

Naomi Osaka, tennis player

Alexi Pappas, distance runner

Katy Perry, musician

Michael Phelps, swimmer

Britney Spears, musician

James Taylor, musician

Kendrick Lamar, rapper

Oprah Winfrey, talk show host and actress

Bipolar Disorder

An individual with bipolar disorder alternates between two "poles" of emotion, namely depression (low periods) and mania (high periods of overactivity, paired with either extreme happiness or irritability). Bipolar disorder is less common than major depression, but still affects approximately 4% of Americans at some time in their lives.

Let's consider Whitney and her mom's experience of bipolar disorder.

Whitney, age 14, was excited for spring break because her mom, Yolanda, had promised to re-decorate her bedroom. The first few days were awesome. Yolanda and Whitney went to several stores and purchased a few bedspread options and accessories. Whitney was amazed at how much money her mom spent and was somewhat embarrassed by her demanding behavior with the salesperson. Whitney noticed that her mom stayed up several nights in a row getting ready. She took down the old curtains, prepared the walls for painting, and searched online for cute wall hangings. Although it was fun, Whitney was a bit annoyed because her mom never stopped talking and was pretty tense.

Yolanda and Whitney had agreed to start painting the bedroom on Wednesday. However, when the day arrived, Yolanda didn't get out of bed. In fact, she seemed pretty out of it. She spent most of the rest of the week sleeping and playing games on her tablet. She didn't shower or get dressed, and looked very sad. Whitney was confused and angry that her mom could disappoint her so much. Dealing with her mom's mood swings had been difficult in the past, but this time really hurt.

Now, Whitney's room is a mess, the bedspreads are still in the bag, and her mom is in bed. Whitney is frustrated and anxious; she just does not know what to do. Yolanda's behavior is hard to predict. She is up and energetic one week, and then down and withdrawn for the next couple months. These symptoms may be consistent with bipolar disorder.

As described in the preceding section, when people are depressed, they may experience the following:

- Feel very sad or down

- Lose interest in fun activities

- Feel tired and sleep more or less than usual

- Lose their appetite

- Struggle to concentrate and make decisions

- Think about death

Mania, on the other hand, can involve the following symptoms:

- Need little sleep

- Be very active or energetic

- Feel "on top of the world" or irritable

- Act in potentially risky ways

- Talk more than usual, often in a pressured, rapid manner

Everybody has good days when they feel happy, optimistic, and engaged with life. That is different from a manic episode. Mania usually creates problems for people with their relationships, work, or school. The symptoms last at least several days and may continue for weeks or months. Some people enjoy the happiness and increased energy during manic periods, while other people find it upsetting and disorienting. Either way, these revved-up behaviors can be confusing and overwhelming for people around them.

Different types of bipolar disorder vary in the severity and duration of the symptoms. However, everyone managing bipolar disorder experiences big changes in motivation, sleep patterns, activity levels, and mood. Details about the different types of bipolar disorder are beyond the scope of this book, but check out the Resource List on page 133 if you wish to learn more.

How about you?

Do you notice your parent experiencing any signs of bipolar disorder? If so, which ones? _____

_____

Which symptoms are toughest for you? _____

_____

How do you feel when your parent is struggling with these problems? The list of feelings on page 130 may be helpful. _____

_____

Famous People With Bipolar Disorder

Mariah Carey, musician

Jim Carrey, actor

Mel Gibson, actor

Selena Gomez, musician

Halsey, musician

Demi Lovato, musician

Bebe Rexha, musician

Ben Stiller, comedian

Sting, musician

Jean-Claude Van Damme, actor

Schizophrenia

People managing schizophrenia may hear, see, or feel things that other people do not. They may hold beliefs that are not based in reality, and they may struggle with concentrating, making decisions, and relating to other people. Schizophrenia-spectrum disorders (an umbrella term that includes both schizophrenia and schizoaffective disorder, a related disorder that also includes mood symptoms like depression or mania) affect approximately 2% of Americans at some point in their lives.

Let's meet Michael and his eighth-grade son, Nate.

Michael is a 44-year-old divorced father who works the night shift at a local convenience store. Michael hears voices that others do not hear, and he worries that customers are whispering about him behind his back. His supervisor recently commented that Michael talks to himself which disturbs his coworkers.

Nate, Michael's son, lives primarily with his mom but often spends weekends with his dad. Nate has always thought that his dad was a bit different from other parents, but lately things have deteriorated. Not only does his dad mutter under his breath, now he seems withdrawn…almost like he's in his own world. Nate also notices that his dad laughs inappropriately when difficult topics arise, such as grandma's recent cancer diagnosis. Nate is confused and scared. He talks to his older sister, but she doesn't know what to do either.

Michael is experiencing several symptoms that may be part of schizophrenia. These problems are affecting him both at work and with his family.

Schizophrenia can involve the following symptoms:

- Hold beliefs that are not grounded in reality (**delusions**), such as:
  - Believing they are famous or have special abilities
  - Experiencing paranoia, being overly suspicious and doubting others' motives and trustworthiness

- Experience things through their senses that aren't there (**hallucinations**), such as:
  - Seeing people or objects that are not present
  - Hearing voices or sounds that others do not hear

- Avoid social interactions because being around other people takes a lot of energy or feels uncomfortable

- Struggle with concentration

- Speak in a confusing manner and display unusual emotions, such as:
  - Jumping from one topic to another
  - Using made-up words or phrases that others don't understand
  - Displaying few emotions, or showing feelings that don't match the situation

How about you?

Does your parent experience any of these symptoms of schizophrenia? If so, which ones? _____

_____

Which symptoms are toughest for you? _____

_____

How do you feel when your parent is struggling with these problems? _____

_____

_____

Famous People With Schizophrenia

Lionel Aldridge, football player

Aaron Carter, rapper

Fred Frese, psychologist

Peter Green, musician

Sasha Lane, actress

John Nash, mathematician

Elyn Saks, author & law professor

Andrew Toles, baseball player

Brian Wilson, musician

To learn more about major depression, bipolar disorder, and schizophrenia, check out the Resource List on page 133.

Part Three of this book provides tools for how teens like Akira, Whitney, and Nate can cope with these challenging family situations.

CHAPTER 4

Causes of Mental Illness

Many myths exist about what causes mental illness, such as the idea that emotional problems result from a character flaw or personal weakness. You may have heard such misinformation from friends, movies, or social media. These myths can be confusing and damaging. Sadly, they can perpetuate inaccurate beliefs and contribute to stigma, an important topic discussed in Chapter 13.

<table>
<tr><td rowspan="3">How about you?</td><td>What have you heard from other people about the causes of mental illness?

_____

_____</td></tr>
<tr><td>What do you think causes mental illness? _____

_____

_____</td></tr>
</table>

Although scientists continue to study the causes of mental illness, we still don't fully understand who will develop an illness and what precisely causes them to do so. It's generally not just one issue that causes an illness to emerge. Instead, there are typically several risk factors that accumulate and can increase one's vulnerability to mental health problems.

Some teens wonder if they caused their parent to develop a mental illness, asking themselves, *If only I hadn't fought so much with my brother which stressed my mom out,* or *If only I hadn't gotten into so much trouble at school which upset my dad immensely.* If you find yourself asking these questions, remember Fact #2: *There is nothing you did to cause your parent to have a mental illness.*

In this chapter we explore how mental illness is caused by a combination of heredity and other risk factors, including additional biological issues, life experiences, and social factors. We also examine the importance of protective factors—things that can decrease one's level of risk.

Heredity

The genes you inherited from your parents affect many traits, such as eye color and hair texture. They also influence your risk for physical health conditions like cancer and diabetes. However, just because you inherit certain genes does not mean you'll develop the condition. You have an increased risk, but the chance of your having these diseases is affected by many other factors such as your eating habits, level of physical activity, and use of nicotine and other substances.

It's the same with mental illness. Here's what we know from research:

- Having a parent or sibling with a mental illness can increase your risk of developing an illness

- Most people with mental illness in the family do not develop emotional problems themselves

- Many people who develop a mental illness don't have any family history of mental health problems—so it's clearly not all about heredity

Chapter 16 explores how to manage your personal risk for developing a mental illness. We offer strategies to strengthen your mental health and tools to cope with challenging life circumstances.

Risk Factors

Beyond inherited genes, many other factors can increase the likelihood of developing a mental illness. The risk may be greater for people who experience several of the following:

Risk Factors		
Biological Factors	**Life Experiences**	**Social Factors**
Imbalance in brain chemicals, often neurotransmitters such as dopamine or serotonin	Chaotic family environment (e.g., parental substance abuse, family violence, child abuse or neglect, parental incarceration)	Poverty, unemployment, or lack of consistent access to food
Brain injury		Unstable housing or unsafe living environment
Some physical health conditions (e.g., diabetes, stroke, heart attack)	Loss of a loved one (e.g., death, divorce)	Stigma and discrimination (e.g., regarding race, disability, sexual orientation, gender identity)
Big changes in hormone levels such as after having a baby	Stressful early life experiences such as bullying	War or community violence
	Trauma	Social isolation or loneliness

As you can see, there are many different factors that can increase an individual's risk for developing a mental illness.

Protective Factors

Beyond risk factors, it's equally important to understand protective factors, namely things that can buffer individuals from having difficulties. They can also improve the person's ability to cope with challenges when they do arise.

There are many different protective factors, and they can be aspects of the individual, their network of family and friends, and their broader community and culture.

Protective Factors		
Individual	**Family and Friends**	**Community and Culture**
Regular physical activity	Supportive parents	Living in a safe neighborhood
Sufficient sleep	Positive family relationships, including with siblings	Feeling connected to the community
Healthy diet	Strong connections with friends	Access to healthcare and support services
Optimism and hope for the future	Participating in activities with others, such as sports, clubs, or religious/spiritual activities	Access to parks and areas of water such as lakes, ponds, rivers
Sense of purpose in life		
High self-esteem		Strong ties to cultural identity
Avoiding high-risk use of alcohol and drugs	Having a mentor or another supportive adult actively engaged in your life	Connection to cultural traditions and values, such as a focus on service, loyalty, sense of belonging, hope
Use of healthy coping skills		
Willingness to ask for help		

Obviously, none of these protective factors can prevent difficulties from arising, but they can make the road a bit easier and more manageable.

The reality is that most people go through tough times and face stressful events. That's part of being human. Each person has a unique blend of risk factors and protective factors, some of which may change over time. Although some risk factors cannot be modified, people can learn skills and connect with resources that strengthen their ability to cope with hardships. Many of the tools and skills in Part Three of this book can be protective factors for you as you navigate the journey of parental mental illness in your family.

CHAPTER 5

Problems That Can Arise After Trauma

While there are some similarities between posttraumatic stress disorder (PTSD) and the mental illnesses discussed in the preceding chapters, PTSD does have some distinct differences.

Before focusing specifically on PTSD, this chapter considers some broader concepts about trauma.

The Facts About Trauma

Some people use the word "traumatic" to describe distressing experiences such as failing a test or breaking up with someone. Although such things can be extremely upsetting, the word "trauma" in the mental health field has a narrower definition. It refers to *exposure to death (threatened or actual), serious injury, or sexual violence.* The person could have experienced the event themselves, watched it happen to someone else, or learned that it happened to a close family member/friend.

Most people experience a traumatic event during their lifetime. Although the media depicts stories of horrible tragedies every day, a great deal of trauma is kept private, hidden in survivors' minds and bodies.

Trauma can be experienced in a wide variety of situations such as military combat, natural disasters (earthquakes, floods, hurricanes, tornadoes), acts of terror, serious car accidents, school shootings, family violence, rape or sexual assault, abuse (physical, sexual, emotional), and community violence (riots, gang fights). First responders, such as firefighters and police, regularly encounter dangerous situations, and this repeated exposure can also be a form of trauma.

Immediately after experiencing a trauma, many people:

- Think a lot about the event

- Feel nervous or worried

- Have nightmares or difficulty sleeping

- Feel in a daze

- Struggle to concentrate

Fortunately, these problems usually become less intense over time and often disappear. *The large majority of people who experience traumatic events do not develop PTSD or other long-term problems.* They are resilient and able to draw upon their existing support network, healthy coping tools, and personal strength. Although the trauma survivor no doubt thinks about the event and experiences lingering feelings, they are not overwhelmed or paralyzed by the memories or emotions; they do not feel haunted or defined by the event.

How about you?

Do you know what traumatic experience(s) your parent has had? If so, name them here if you wish: _____

_____

If your parent's trauma occurred since you've been old enough to remember what they were like before, how have they changed? _____

_____

When the Problems Continue

Although most survivors feel much better within the first several weeks after the trauma, some are haunted by the event for many years. As seen in this image, many different problems can emerge, including PTSD. Other common issues include anxiety, depression, relationship problems, addictions (see Chapter 7 for more information), and moral injury (shame or guilt about having done or seen something that violated one's morals or core beliefs). Many people experience several of these problems simultaneously. For example, over half of all people with PTSD also have major depression.

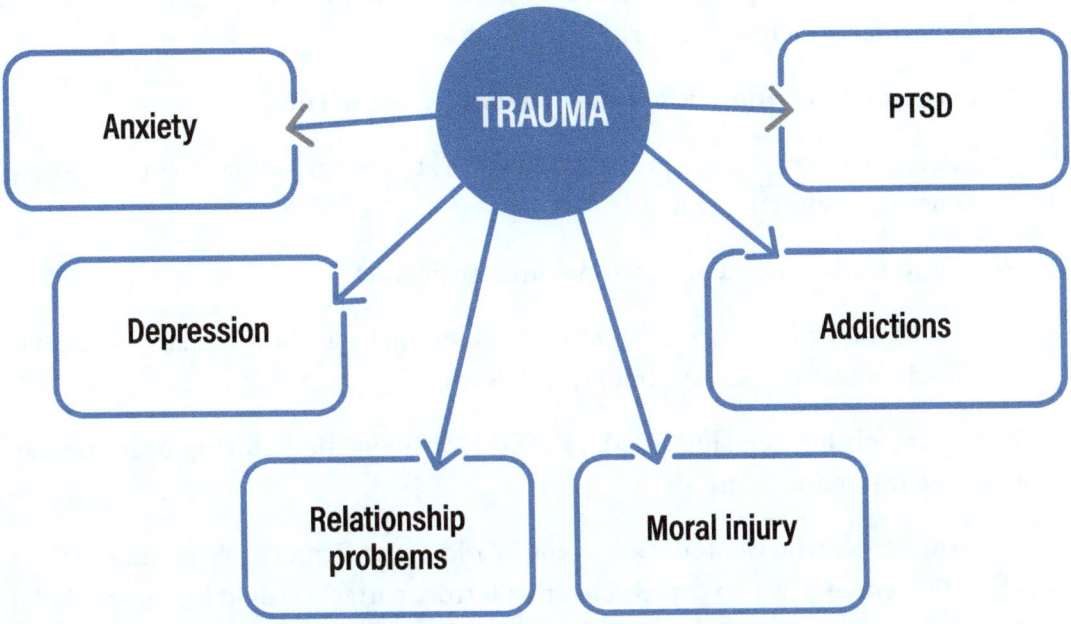

Risk Factors for Developing Problems After Trauma

How can you predict who will develop lasting problems? That's a common question but one with no clear answers. It is actually impossible to know how a specific person will respond to trauma. However, understanding risk factors can be helpful.

Research has examined a wide range of risk factors which can fall in these four categories:

- The nature of the trauma

- The individual's past experiences and well-being

- What happened after the trauma, including reactions from family/friends

- Genetic factors

The Nature of the Trauma

People are more likely to develop mental health problems if they:

- **Were very close to and personally involved with the traumatic event**

  o Firefighters and police officers are intimately involved in dangerous situations which may increase their risk of difficulties.

- **Were exposed to traumatic events for a long period of time**

  o People who survive years of abuse may be at greater risk than people who experienced an isolated incident.

- **Were physically injured or saw someone else be hurt**

  o Emergency room nurses can struggle emotionally as they regularly witness high levels of distress, serious injury, and death.

- **Felt extremely helpless, horrified, or afraid for their safety during or immediately after the traumatic event**

  o The people who went to work at the World Trade Center on September 11, 2001, could never have predicted that terrorist attacks would kill nearly 3,000 individuals and injure over 6,000 others that day. When the towers were struck, thousands of people experienced panic and terror; many witnessed mass devastation and casualties as they tried to evacuate the towers, get to safety, and communicate with loved ones.

- **Felt betrayed by someone they trusted**

  o Many people who have been sexually abused by clergy feel betrayed by the individual and sometimes by the church in general. Similarly, people mistreated by a relative may feel betrayed by the family. Being abused by someone you know and trust can provoke very complex feelings.

The Individual's Past Experiences and Well-Being

An individual's past life experiences and overall well-being before the trauma are related to their chance of developing mental health problems. For example, if the survivor had a pre-existing mental illness, they would be at higher risk for having problems afterwards.

Furthermore, people who have experienced any trauma in the past—including childhood trauma—are more likely to have difficulties. For example, consider Louis's situation:

> *Louis, a French teacher at the local high school, was devastated when a shooting occurred at his school a year ago. Although several students were badly hurt, Louis was not injured. He had nightmares for several months after the shooting and sometimes dreaded going to school. Things got easier as time went on and he focused on enjoying and supporting his students.*
>
> *Last week Louis was seriously injured while participating in a protest in his community. He may be at higher risk of experiencing mental health problems due to the combined impact of the school shooting and recent injury.*

What Happened After the Trauma, Including Reactions From Family/Friends

What transpires in the aftermath of the event can really impact the survivor's recovery. People who have good coping skills tend to do better emotionally. Knowing how to get through rough times and deal with strong emotions can decrease the chance of developing long-term problems. On the other hand, people who tend to isolate from others, avoid facing their fears, or abuse substances may have a higher risk of struggling emotionally.

Furthermore, survivors with caring people in their lives are less likely to develop long-term difficulties. Having compassionate, nonjudgmental, and encouraging family and friends can help the survivor reconnect with others, feel less alone, and heal from the trauma. In contrast, survivors who lack support or are blamed by others are more likely to struggle. For example, let's look at Margaret's experience.

> *Margaret was sexually assaulted after leaving a fraternity party with a man she thought she could trust. She was overwhelmed with strong feelings—rage, fear, and guilt. Although most of her friends were very supportive, she was deeply hurt by her parents who asked judgmental questions such as, "How much were you drinking?"*

and "What were you wearing?" They also told her what to do, such as, "You really should report this to the police" and "You need to go to counseling." Over time, as the event continued to haunt Margaret, her parents said insensitive things like, "You really should be over this by now" and "You just need to get on with your life."

Unsupportive and critical reactions, such as what Margaret received from her parents, can undermine the survivor's sense of control. Research has found that such hurtful feedback from family and friends can increase psychological distress and hinder healing and recovery. Margaret would have appreciated supportive comments from her parents, such as, *"We hate that this happened to you and are here for you no matter what. It's not your fault, and it took a lot of courage for you to share this with us."*

Genetic Factors

Research with twins and other cutting-edge studies from around the world suggests that genetics may play a significant role in who develops PTSD after trauma. In fact, some studies show that the contribution of genes/heredity is just as strong for PTSD as it is with other mental illnesses such as major depression. Much more research is needed in this area, but it's hopeful that improving our understanding of the role of genetics will guide the development of personalized treatments for trauma survivors.

Having reviewed a range of possible reactions to trauma and risk factors for greater difficulties, in the next chapter we take a deeper dive into one possible outcome of trauma, namely PTSD.

CHAPTER 6

One Possible Outcome of Trauma: PTSD

As discussed in the previous chapter, posttraumatic stress disorder (PTSD) is a mental illness that can emerge after experiencing a traumatic event. Approximately 1 in 14 people (7%) develops PTSD at some time during their lives.

Just like with other illnesses, the experience of PTSD can be quite different from one person to another. Your parent may have many of the symptoms described in this chapter, or just a few. One person may struggle with the problems for many years, while someone else might recover quickly. Sometimes people do well for a long time and then have symptoms return after a stressful experience or big life change such as retirement.

Despite looking at serious mental illness (schizophrenia, depression, and bipolar disorder) and PTSD separately in Part Two of this book, they're actually quite intertwined:

- People with a serious mental illness are at higher risk than the general population for experiencing trauma and developing PTSD.
- About 75% of people with PTSD have another mental health problem, with depression and alcohol/drug abuse being common co-existing conditions.

Let's meet Greg and his son, Paul.

> Greg joined the Army right out of high school. After serving stateside for a few years, he deployed to a combat zone in the Middle East and was responsible for a large group of soldiers. One night Greg made the difficult decision to send some of his troops ahead in a risky surveillance mission, and several soldiers lost their lives. He has regretted that decision every day of his life. Greg was also seriously wounded in that conflict, and received a medical discharge from the Army.
>
> For the first few years after getting home, Greg kept busy putting in long hours at work, and seldom talked about his combat experience. He showed up as much as he could for his wife and son, Paul, including coaching Paul's soccer team.
>
> Greg and his wife grew distant in the years following his return from deployment, and she eventually filed for divorce. Since that time, Greg's nightmares have gotten worse, and memories of that day in combat haunt him frequently. He gets angry quickly and doesn't feel close to anyone. He feels nervous in large groups and cannot tolerate busy places like the mall. He often wonders why his good friends were killed but he survived. He quit coaching Paul's soccer team, which was a huge disappointment for his son. Greg drinks heavily many nights a week, and worries he may lose his job due to calling in sick so often.
>
> Paul, now 18, resents his mom for breaking up the family and the military for what happened to his dad. He misses the gentle, playful father he remembers from childhood. Although Paul feels sorry for his dad, he doesn't know how to help. Paul feels alone and heartbroken. It's hard that Greg doesn't attend Paul's senior year activities. Paul had planned to follow his dad's and grandpa's footsteps and join the Army himself—but seeing his dad struggle so much, he isn't sure anymore.

Greg is experiencing several symptoms that may be consistent with PTSD, and his difficulties are affecting his work, marriage, and relationship with his son.

There are four major categories of symptoms in PTSD. The mnemonic RAIN* can help to remember them:

- **R**eliving the trauma in various ways
- **A**voiding reminders of the trauma

- **I**rritability, insomnia, and feeling on edge

- **N**egative thoughts and feelings

* Special thanks to Dr. Alan "Dutch" Doerman, Retired U.S. Air Force Colonel, for allowing us to use this acronym he created.

Reliving the Trauma

Survivors may relive (or re-experience) the traumatic event in a variety of ways:

- People may have upsetting **dreams or nightmares** of the event and **intrusive memories** during the day (thoughts or images that come into their minds, often for no clear reason). In fact, over 70% of people with PTSD experience nightmares. Some trauma survivors fear going to sleep because of the possibility of bad dreams.

- Trauma survivors are often upset by **triggers** or reminders of the event. Triggers can be places, conversations, and thoughts that are somehow connected to the traumatic event; they can cause emotional distress (e.g., fear, anxiety, sadness, anger) and physical reactions (e.g., nausea, increased heart rate, headache, pain).

- Sometimes people act or feel as if the trauma is happening again—a frightening experience called a **flashback**. When having the flashback, the person truly believes that they are back in that situation and that it is occurring again.

Avoiding Reminders of the Trauma

A significant component of PTSD is avoidance, which can occur in several ways:

- Survivors may try to **avoid thoughts, feelings, and memories** of the trauma. Because the trauma was so painful, survivors may work hard to distance themselves from the memories. Some survivors engage in addictive behavior, such as abusing alcohol or drugs, as a way to stay away from the painful memories and feelings. (See Chapter 7 for more on addictions.)

Avoidance is a core symptom of PTSD.

Because the experience of trauma involves a loss of control, avoiding triggers can make a lot of sense.

However, doing so can contribute to isolation and missing out on meaningful activities.

- People may actively avoid **places, activities, and people** that remind them of the trauma. Survivors may change their routines such as not going to certain parts of town. Others avoid movies, news broadcasts, and social media related to the trauma.

Irritability, Insomnia, and Feeling on Edge

Some trauma survivors feel uptight and restless much of the time, making it hard to relax and focus on everyday activities. For instance:

- Many people with PTSD tend to be **irritable** and have **angry outbursts**. Small daily hassles such as encountering heavy traffic can produce strong emotional reactions— sometimes rage that is out of proportion to the situation. The anger can arise quickly, and is sometimes misdirected and taken out on the people they love. The intense emotions are understandable because trauma usually involves being threatened, hurt, or taken advantage of—all situations that can evoke rage.

  Note: Your parent's anger may be intense and frightening for you and others in the home, including pets. It can be hard to know how to manage those situations. If your parent has angry outbursts, please see Chapter 15 for tips on how to cope. PTSD is not an acceptable excuse for scaring or harming other people. You deserve to feel safe in your house.

- Survivors may experience **insomnia** and get little quality rest. Trauma memories can be more vivid and intense at night without the distractions of everyday life, making it hard to relax and fall asleep. As noted earlier, bad dreams can disrupt sleep, both for the survivor and bed partner.

- Some survivors are **hypervigilant,** meaning they are on high alert for possible danger or threat. Although being very aware of your environment can be helpful in situations such as combat, some survivors struggle to relax, even in safe places. For example, they may sit with their backs to the wall in restaurants to monitor their surroundings. In addition, they may become quite **startled** if someone approaches unexpectedly. Because of both these factors, some survivors avoid social situations, which can increase their isolation.

Negative Thoughts and Feelings

Trauma can darken the survivor's overall perspective on life and view of themselves and others, all of which can have negative impacts on relationships. For example:

- Some survivors shut down emotionally to avoid the pain related to the trauma. In doing so, however, they can become **numb**. They may also **feel distant from other people** and have a **hard time experiencing and expressing happy or loving feelings.**

- A trauma survivor may **lose interest in activities** they used to enjoy. Nothing feels fun or rewarding anymore, so they withdraw from people and hobbies that historically had offered some meaning and connection.

- Some may struggle with an **overall negative view** of themselves and **chronic painful feelings** such as guilt, shame, or fear. People who have experienced life-threatening situations involving other people may develop survivor guilt, a painful emotion in which they wonder why they lived through the trauma when others did not.

> Trauma survivors describe how they build "walls" around themselves that protect them from strong emotions and from being close to people.
>
> Although the survivor may want to feel close to their family, being vulnerable can feel uncomfortable and risky.

Remember that no one experiences every symptom of PTSD, and each person's reaction to trauma is unique. Greg dealt with many of these issues, and they affected his relationship with his wife and son. Let's consider your own parent's experience:

How about you?

Which of the symptoms described in this chapter do you observe in your parent? Of course, some symptoms cannot be observed by other people, but you likely notice some behaviors. Consider the four RAIN categories:

- **Reliving the Trauma**: Are you aware of specific triggers that upset your parent? If so, what are they?_____

_____

- **Avoidance**: Do you notice your parent avoiding specific situations or places? If so, what?_____

_____

- **Irritability and Being on Edge**: Have you observed your parent being cranky or hypervigilant (highly alert to potential threat or danger)? Or perhaps having a strong startle response? What have you seen?

_____

_____

- **Negative Thoughts and Feelings**: Is your parent emotionally distant? Do you notice that they have withdrawn from activities they used to enjoy?

_____

_____

How do you feel when your parent is struggling with these problems? _____

_____

_____

In Part Three of this book, we will explore ways of coping with difficult emotions, people who may be able to help you, and ways to strengthen your relationship with your parent. We'll also examine the importance of your continuing to live your best life and doing things you enjoy, even when your parent is struggling.

Famous People Who Have Experienced PTSD

Lady Gaga, musician

Whoopi Goldberg, actress

Ariana Grande, singer

Darrell Hammond, comedian

Prince Harry, royalty

Mick Jagger, singer

Shia LaBeouf, actor

Clint Malarchuk, hockey player

Tracy Morgan, comedian/actor

Gabrielle Union, actress

Although this chapter focused on having a parent who has experienced trauma, it's possible that you may have experienced a highly upsetting event as well. Perhaps nobody knows about the terrible thing that happened to you, or maybe your trauma is public and you have gotten counseling. Regardless of your specific situation, we hope that you find healthy ways of coping with your painful feelings. Telling someone about your traumatic event takes a lot of courage, and you may feel better when you allow supportive people to help you heal.

CHAPTER 7

Addictions Including Alcohol and Drug Abuse

Now that we have addressed key issues surrounding both mental illness and trauma/PTSD, Chapters 7 and 8 explore two broad topics, namely **addiction** and **treatment options** for your parent.

Addictions

Many people draw upon healthy coping skills to manage challenging life situations and strong emotions. On the other hand, some use dangerous strategies. Others take typically healthy behaviors to an extreme, such as excessive exercise.

Addiction involves the inability to stop a behavior despite negative consequences. Although some addictive substances or behaviors are safe in moderation, problems can emerge when people need more and more to get the relief or good feelings they crave. As the addiction progresses, the person may feel out of control. They may compulsively spend a lot of time, energy, and money on the behavior. People may feel desperate for something to numb their pain, even for just a little while.

When thinking about addictions, drugs and alcohol often come to mind. However, people can become addicted to many things, such as:

Caffeine	Prescribed medications	Exercise	Sex	Gambling
Shopping	Nicotine	Work	Pornography	Video games

The addictive behavior may seem baffling to an outsider who wonders why the person cannot just stop. For the person struggling, however, the behavior may be the best way they know to cope with overwhelming pain, and quitting may seem impossible.

Abuse of Alcohol and Drugs

About 17% of American adults report having a substance use disorder in the past year, defined as ongoing use of alcohol or drugs despite harmful consequences. Although rates vary globally, substance abuse is a significant problem around the world.

Prevalence of Substance Use Disorder among Adults

- General public: 1 in 6
- People with a serious mental illness: 1 in 4
- People with PTSD: 1 in 2

Furthermore, rates of substance use disorders are higher among people with a serious mental illness. In fact, about 25% of these adults also have an addiction to alcohol or drugs.

Similarly, almost half of people who have PTSD also have problems with alcohol or drugs. While trauma survivors may be trying to distract themselves from painful memories, substances can worsen some PTSD symptoms and cause other physical and mental health problems. Furthermore, alcohol and drug abuse can put people in dangerous situations that may increase their risk of experiencing trauma and potentially developing PTSD.

How about you?

Does your parent use alcohol or other drugs to self-medicate or numb themself? If so, what do you notice? _____

_____

_____

How does their use affect you? _____

_____

_____

Alcohol and drugs (including marijuana) can intensify many symptoms of mental illness. For example, alcohol is a depressant and can worsen sadness and disrupt sleep in people managing depression. Also, the medications used to treat mental illness may not work as well because of the alcohol or drugs in the person's system. Bottom line: the combination of mental illness and substance abuse can result in people having a considerably more difficult road.

Let's look at Amanda and her son, Sayer, to think more about the relationship between emotional problems and substance use disorders.

Amanda is a single mom who is raising her son, Sayer, a high-school senior. Her husband died from liver cancer three years ago, and she has been struggling emotionally ever since. She misses her husband dearly, doesn't have much energy, and feels depressed and lonely. As for Sayer, he was devastated when his dad died. He finds it helpful to talk with his uncle, both about their grief as well as the fishing trips they all enjoyed together.

Recently, Amanda was in a bad car accident in which the other driver was seriously injured. Since then, she has felt tense and has been having nightmares of the accident. She's quite tired in the morning, and is late to work more often than not. She spends much of her free time scrolling on social media. Although Amanda has always enjoyed a drink before dinner, she has started drinking more heavily since the accident. On the weekends, she spends the afternoon at the local sports bar, and then retreats to her bedroom when she gets home. At night when she can't sleep, she has several drinks to relax.

Things have gotten worse for Sayer at home since his mom's accident. She is often cranky and doesn't seem to care about his activities. She barely leaves the house, other than to go to work and the bar. She doesn't cook much, so Sayer gets a lot of take-out meals. Last week Sayer had friends over to the house. When his mom got drunk and obnoxious, he was furious. He felt humiliated. He didn't know what to do, so he just asked his friends to leave.

Why Does Amanda Turn to Alcohol?

Although alcohol probably serves many functions for Amanda, she mainly drinks to:

Escape sadness and bad memories

Amanda has felt depressed since her husband died; her life just feels empty without him. On top of that is the car accident, and she is struggling with many symptoms of PTSD including significant guilt that the other driver was seriously injured. Amanda finds that alcohol "takes the edge off" both the grief and painful memories. Although she enjoys the temporary escape from reality, the problems and feelings are still there when the alcohol wears off—compounded by regret for drinking so much and not spending time with Sayer.

Fall asleep

Because missing her husband is worse at night, Amanda drinks to help fall asleep. While alcohol helps her get to sleep, she doesn't get good quality rest. She often feels hungover, irritable, and tired the next morning, which sometimes results in her starting to drink early in the day—a vicious cycle.

Relax

Amanda believes that alcohol is the only thing that can help her get through the day. She feels most relaxed when she's had a few shots at the bar and loses herself in watching a good basketball game. Sayer notices that although Mom is often crabby and high-strung, she is calmer after a few drinks.

Avoid feeling lonely

Although Amanda has gotten to know a few people at the bar, no one really knows what's going on in her life. She feels lost, but finds alcohol can numb her loneliness.

What Problems Might Amanda Face if She Continues to Abuse Alcohol?

Although Amanda is probably doing her best to cope, more difficulties may arise if she continues drinking heavily. People with a substance use disorder often have problems in the following areas:

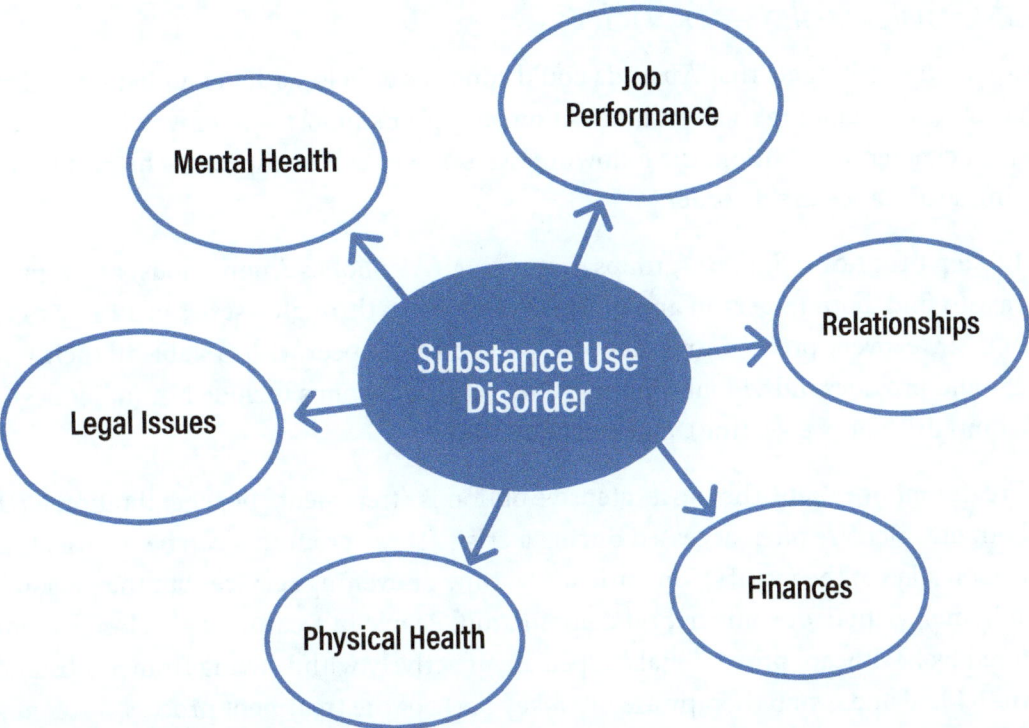

- **Job performance**: Tardiness, difficulty concentrating, poor performance, being fired

- **Relationships**: Frequent conflict, loss of trust and respect, losing friends, marital problems

- **Finances**: Spending a lot of money on alcohol/drugs, not paying bills on time, loss of income from not working, bankruptcy

- **Physical health**: Weight loss or gain, liver damage, increased risk of heart disease and some cancers

- **Legal issues**: Being arrested, fines and legal fees, losing driver's license, being incarcerated

- **Mental health**: Depression, anxiety, irritability, sleep problems, shame, guilt

What Could Help Amanda?

There are many treatments that Amanda could consider to help with her addiction and mental health problems, including therapy, medication, and peer support—all of which are described in the next chapter. In addition, the following two services can be especially helpful for people managing a substance use disorder:

> **12-step programs:** Support groups such as AA (Alcoholics Anonymous) are popular and easy to find, both in person and online. People work through a series of 12 steps as part of their recovery process, and many have a sponsor (a peer who is stable in their recovery and provides individual support). Other similar groups include NA (narcotics), OA (compulsive or over-eating), and GA (gambling).

> **Treatment or rehab:** The most intensive option is "treatment" or rehabilitation ("rehab"), both of which are often accessed during a crisis. These programs can be inpatient (the person stays at the facility), outpatient (daytime or evening services but the person lives at home), virtual, or some hybrid combination. People in treatment are closely monitored by healthcare professionals, especially if actively withdrawing from a substance. Individual and group therapy are often key parts of the treatment process.

How Might Sayer Be Feeling?

Sayer is probably experiencing a lot of feelings—confusion, anger, sadness, worry, powerlessness, and more. He misses his dad and feels pretty alone. His mom is in the throes of an addiction on top of her grief and sadness, and she doesn't have much time or energy for him. It seems she prefers drinking or hibernating in her bedroom to spending time with her son. Sayer has learned that he cannot depend on his mom because she doesn't consistently follow through on her word. He is also mortified when his mom is drunk in front of his friends. He tends to stay away from the house as much as possible, and he stopped inviting people over.

Sayer knows that alcoholism runs in his family, as his grandma and aunt also drink very heavily. He recently started having a few beers with his buddies, and sometimes finds it hard to stop after one or two. Because of his family history, he worries he might develop problems with alcohol himself.

What Could Help Sayer?

Sayer may benefit from talking with other teens whose parent abuses alcohol or drugs. Just as AA exists for the person with the addiction, there are support groups for spouses/partners and teenagers as well. Perhaps you have heard of Al-Anon, a 12-step program for adults who love someone with an alcohol problem. There is a similar program for teenagers named Alateen, which offers free, confidential support groups where teens talk to other youth whose parent abuses alcohol or drugs. Sayer might find it helpful to learn how others deal with the stresses of having a parent with an addiction to alcohol.

Alateen offers free support groups for teens.

To find virtual or in-person meetings near you, see their website: https://al-anon.org

If Amanda seeks professional help, Sayer may have the opportunity to be involved in a family meeting. He might also participate in family therapy where he and his mom could discuss how her difficulties affect both of them, and how they can work together as a team.

Finally, Sayer is right that there's a strong hereditary component for substance use disorders. Therefore, he may want to be careful about his drinking, both now and in the future.

CHAPTER 8

Professionals and Treatments That Can Help Your Parent: The Hope of Recovery

Before diving into this chapter's topic of professionals and treatment options, we want to emphasize two important subjects, namely **recovery** and **resilience**.

Recovery Is Possible

As noted in previous chapters, the course of mental illness is unique for each person. Doctors and scientists are working hard to identify early warning signs and intervene quickly when people first experience symptoms.

Many people managing a mental illness improve over time. About half of people diagnosed with PTSD no longer meet criteria for the illness after two years. Similarly, research that followed people living with schizophrenia over two decades found that about 25% no longer had symptoms; they were doing well with their relationships, job, and community activities. Beyond that 25%, many more people had considerably improved, having positive social connections and mild symptoms.

Some people have a more chronic course of illness, such as recurring episodes of depression or mania. However, they can often manage their symptoms effectively, supported by many of the treatments described in this chapter. The ongoing development of new medications and therapies is reason for hope.

> Recovery is not an end point and does not necessarily mean that all symptoms completely go away.
>
> Rather, it is a journey that includes good as well as challenging days.

People who would have been limited by their illness in the past now lead productive, meaningful lives.

The possibility of **recovery** exists for everyone. As opposed to thinking about recovery as an endpoint associated with stopping alcohol or drug use, this term has a somewhat different meaning in the context of mental illness. Here, recovery is a process marked by hope, as people work to: improve health, move toward personal goals, take personal responsibility, and use one's skills in a meaningful way.

Each person's recovery process is unique, but it often involves accepting one's illness and making healthy choices such as the following:

- Communicating openly and honestly with doctors and therapists

- Staying connected to other people and avoiding isolation

- Getting regular check-ups

- Making healthy food choices

- Getting regular physical activity

- Avoiding or minimizing use of alcohol and other substances

- Getting sufficient sleep

As part of recovery, many people help others who are dealing with a mental illness by providing support and friendship. Having a sense of community and feeling connected to other people can be incredibly important and healing.

Recognizing Your Parent's Strength and Resilience

Your parent may have been through a great deal in their journey with mental illness, including many different medications, various therapies, hospitalizations, alcohol or drug treatment programs, and more. Through all of this, perhaps you've come to appreciate that your parent is **resilient**—they keep trying, even when it's hard. Sometimes it may take a huge amount of effort for them to just get out of bed or make dinner, but they keep showing up.

Maybe you realize that your parent is strong and can handle a lot. You might admire their sense of humor, or how they draw upon a strong foundation of faith. You may recognize that managing a mental illness takes a lot of courage and perseverance. Focusing on these positive qualities in your parent can give you hope.

How about you?

What do you see your parent doing that may be helping their recovery? Attending a support group? Regular exercise or healthy eating? _____

_____

Recovery does not happen in isolation. Who is supporting your parent in their recovery? This may include family, friends, peers, and professionals. _____

_____

What have you noticed about your parent's resilience? What do you think has kept them going despite challenges? (it may be you, by the way!)_____

_____

Now, let's turn to exploring who can help your parent as well as treatment options for mental illness.

Professionals and Treatments That Can Help Your Parent

Who Can Help Your Parent?

While family members and friends are often helpful members of a support network, mental health clinicians are usually an important part of the team as well.

When your parent seeks professional help, it's important to find the right providers. Many specialists have formal training in understanding and treating mental illness and trauma. Your parent's treatment team may include one or more of the following:

- **Psychiatrist/psychiatric nurse** who prescribes medications and offers brief counseling

- **Psychologist** who provides more in-depth talk therapy and psychological testing

- **Social worker or counselor** who offers counseling and helps find community resources

- **Marriage and family therapist** who provides therapy for the entire family to strengthen relationships

- **Peer support specialist** who has personal experience of mental illness or trauma and has formal training, enabling them to support others and serve as a role model

- **Alcohol and drug counselor** who helps with making changes in addictive behavior

- **Spiritual leader/minister/clergy** who supports people with the religious or spiritual aspects of mental illness and trauma, including moral injury (shame or guilt often experienced by trauma survivors about having done something that violated their morals or core beliefs)

- **Case manager** who coordinates care

- **Primary care doctor** who manages overall care

What Can Help Your Parent?

As noted in Fact #5, many treatment options exist that may help your parent. Living with a mental illness is similar to managing chronic physical problems such as asthma or diabetes. Scientists have yet to discover cures for these diseases. However, with an accurate diagnosis, healthy lifestyle, support from professionals and family/friends, and often regular medications, people with chronic physical and mental health problems can enjoy rich and full lives.

So, what can help your parent? Treatment often involves several elements, including but not limited to:

- Therapy
- Medications
- Peer support
- Family involvement

Therapy

Therapy offers people the opportunity to confide in a trusted professional about feelings, thoughts, and experiences and to learn helpful coping skills. Although talking with friends can be great, therapists are trained to be good listeners, offering undivided attention, an unbiased perspective, and skills for managing symptoms and improving well-being. Therapists are also bound by confidentiality so will keep what is shared private (except for emergency situations such as possible violence, danger, or abuse).* Therapy takes time and courage, and it's crucial to find a therapist that is trustworthy, helpful, and genuinely caring.

* The rules about confidentiality are somewhat different for youth and differ across state and specific situation. If you seek therapy for yourself, it's important to have an open conversation at the beginning about what is and what is not shared with your parents or caregivers.

Beyond talking individually with a therapist, your parent may also benefit from group therapy. Talking with other people living with similar challenges can be helpful, and your parent can be reassured that they are not alone. Couples or family therapy can also be very useful. Both of your parents, and perhaps you as well, can discuss how the mental illness affects your family. Therapists offer skills to help couples/families communicate effectively, improve their relationships, and work together to understand and cope with the illness.

Regardless of the format or specific model, therapy often involves working on the following issues:

- Getting back to enjoyable, meaningful activities instead of isolating

- Learning how to deal with strong feelings and process painful memories instead of avoiding them

- Trying new coping tools to manage symptoms

- Gaining support in making positive lifestyle choices, such as regular physical activity, healthy eating habits, and consistent sleep habits

- Discovering ways to relax

> Courage doesn't always roar. Sometimes it is the quiet voice at the end of the day saying, "I will try again tomorrow."
>
> MaryAnne Radmacher[1]

- Learning strategies for solving problems

- Improving relationships with family and friends

Being in therapy can be hard work. It takes strength to look within yourself, to be vulnerable with another person, and to make changes.

Medication

Your parent may take medication as part of their treatment—perhaps pills, a nasal spray, injections, or some combination. Although medications do not cure mental illness, they can help the symptoms become more manageable and less intense . . . which helps your parent participate more fully in their activities and relationships.

Medications that treat mental illness are safe, and most are not addictive. All medications can have side effects, and each person's body responds differently. For example, after taking a decongestant for a cold, some people feel tired while others feel restless and agitated; it's impossible to predict how an individual will respond. It's the same with mental health medications.

Your parent may have to try several options to find medications that work with few or no unpleasant side effects. Sometimes the nausea, fatigue, weight gain, and headaches go away over time, or other medications are prescribed to minimize them. Fortunately, many options are available, and your parent can collaborate with their doctor/nurse to find a plan that works most effectively, changing doses or medicines over time as needed.

Peer support

When managing a mental illness, connecting with others who truly understand can be enormously helpful. Your parent can feel comforted by talking to peers with similar problems and can simultaneously help others by sharing their own experiences and coping skills.

Peer support is provided in a variety of formats:

Peer support groups: These groups exist for many issues and can help your parent learn new skills and feel less alone. They exist in multiple formats, including in person, online, via mobile apps, and in social media groups. Contact information for several organizations that offer peer support programs is provided in the Resource List on page 133.

Peer support specialists: Specialists are people who have a mental illness, are emotionally stable, and have formal training in helping others. Your parent may benefit from talking individually with someone who can serve as a mentor, trustworthy friend, and source of hope.

Clubhouses: These community centers offer a wide range of services for people living with a mental illness, often including group sessions, case management, advocacy, fieldtrips, and housing assistance. Participants can give and receive support from peers in these relaxed, supportive settings.

Peer support focuses on what's strong, not what's wrong in another's life.[2]

Peer supporters share their own experiences to encourage others.

Across all of these peer support opportunities, people have the chance to talk openly about their feelings and experiences. Although peers do not provide formal therapy, they can be nonjudgmental, encouraging role models for recovery.

Family involvement

Finally, in addition to therapies, medications, and peer support, family participation in treatment can be very useful. You and other family members may read books/websites/blogs, go to counseling yourself, attend support groups, or access mobile apps (such as the Family PTSD Coach developed by clinicians from the VA and Department of Defense). Learning about your parent's difficulties reflects your care for them, and the fact that you're reading this book says a lot!

Beyond couples and family therapy as previously described, another source of great support involves educational classes or support groups. For example, the National Alliance on Mental Illness (NAMI) offers a wide range of free programs for family members and friends.

All 50 United States have NAMI chapters.

You might check into what's available in your state on their website: www.nami.org

In summary, many treatments are available for mental illness, and a variety of professionals may be involved in the care team. First, however, your parent has to be ready and open for help. Let's take a look at some common barriers to seeking treatment for mental health concerns.

Asking for Help

Reaching out for assistance when hurting emotionally is often easier said than done.

How about you?

What do you think makes it hard for people to ask for help for mental health problems? _____

_____

Do you know if your parent has been inconsistent with professional help? For example, have they stopped taking their medication or discontinued therapy?

_____

_____

If so, what has that been like for you? _____

_____

Why Do Many People Living With a Mental Illness Not Get Help?

If your parent is not getting treatment for their mental health problems, they are not alone. Sadly, research has found that only about 60% of American adults living with a mental illness has gotten professional help in the past year. Some have never received treatment, while others discontinue services for a variety of reasons.

Rates of participation in treatment vary widely around the world. Globally, some studies estimate that only about 25% of people living with a mental illness receive treatment, with even lower rates in rural and poverty-stricken regions where services may not be available.

These striking statistics reflect issues at many levels—certainly financial, cultural, societal, access/availability of treatment, and more—all of which can prevent people from getting care.

Consider these common barriers:

- Many people don't know where to go for help.

- The shortage of mental health professionals can make it hard to find a therapist or psychiatry provider. Sadly, long waiting lists are common.

- Mental health services can be expensive, and insurance coverage can vary a lot.

- It takes courage to ask for help. Some people feel embarrassed and ashamed about their problems, and they prefer to keep private matters to themselves. They may be skeptical if anyone can understand or help them.

- People may fear judgment from their family and friends. As we will discuss in Chapter 13, **stigma**—negative attitudes or beliefs—persists surrounding mental illness and seeking help. Further, **discrimination**—unfair treatment due to the illness—can be a significant barrier, such as experiencing negative consequences for one's career. For example, pilots may fear seeking mental health services because they worry they could lose their medical clearance to fly.

- Some cultural groups discourage people from seeking traditional mental health services, tending to draw upon wisdom from elders or faith leaders instead. Going outside one's culture and accessing help from a mental health professional can bring shame to the family.

- Some people living with a mental illness, especially schizophrenia and bipolar disorder, have limited or no insight into their mental health problems. They aren't in denial or being stubborn—they truly do not believe they have an illness. This symptom is called **anosognosia** (*uh-no-sog-NOH-zee-uh*), and it can be frustrating for the family. Because the individual thinks there's nothing wrong with them, they often don't see any reason to take medications, go to therapy, or get other services.

As you can see, there are many barriers that people may need to overcome in order to get help. Understand that it may be hard for your parent to accept that they are struggling and to reach out for treatment. *Dealing with mental illness involves a lot more than just willpower or a positive attitude; it requires courage, persistence, and a significant commitment of time, energy, and money.*

> **Being brave enough to ask for help is a testament to your strength, not a weakness.**
>
> Demi Lovato, musician

So, if your parent is getting professional help, that's very positive and hopeful.

If your parent is not receiving treatment, you may feel powerless and frustrated. It often takes time before people are ready to seek help, and your parent may not be ready to start or resume services. As much as you might encourage them, it is ultimately their decision. Being patient and accepting their timeline can be difficult.

PART THREE

Living With a Parent Who Has a Mental Illness or History of Trauma

CHAPTER 9

How to Identify and Understand Your Feelings

The teenage years can offer many new opportunities, including greater freedom and independence, numerous school and community activities, and a wider peer group. At the same time, adolescence can be hard as you juggle the responsibilities of homework and chores, manage social media, deal with frightening news including school shootings/community violence/war/natural disasters, and make big decisions about your future. It can be a lot.

So, just being a young person these days can be difficult enough—much less adding issues surrounding your parent having a mental illness. Some days you may worry about your mom or dad. The next day you may feel hopeful because they are having a good day. Other times you may be angry and resent the fact that your family is dealing with mental illness. As pointed out in Fact #6, it's normal to experience a wide range of feelings.

Emotions can give you important information, so try to pay attention to what they may be telling you. The word "emotion" has the word "motion" in it—a reminder that feelings can also motivate you to take action.

Let's take a look at some common emotions that teens experience when their parent has a mental illness. Coping with strong feelings begins by recognizing and naming them.

Your Feelings

Turn to the list of emotions on page 130. If you wish, circle those that you have felt recently with respect to your parent.

As you reflect on your emotions, please be kind to yourself. Many people have a pesky internal critic that says: "You shouldn't feel that way!" or "Stop making such a big deal out of it" or "Just get over it!" If these thoughts pop up, take a moment to check in with yourself. Is that critical voice serving you well right now? Probably not.

Instead, ask: "How am I really feeling right now?" Then, *give yourself permission to accept whatever you are experiencing,* such as "Even though this situation/feeling is difficult, this is where I am right now. I can get through this. I know I won't feel this way forever."

Perhaps it's helpful to remember these truths about feelings. They:

- Are part of being human

- Aren't right or wrong—they just are

- Can provide information, including about your values

- Can motivate you to take action

- May feel overwhelming at times, but there are many skills that can help you cope effectively

- Can be tempting to avoid or deny (especially painful ones); however, doing so can keep you stuck. Facing your emotions directly takes courage and can help you to cope and move forward authentically.

The rest of this chapter explores six emotions experienced by many teens whose parent has a mental illness.

Sadness

Caring about someone with a mental illness can bring up a lot of sadness and pain. It can just hurt to see your mom or dad struggling.

Many teens in this situation go through times of being very down or depressed themselves. You may feel:

- Sad that your parent has the illness

- Powerless about how to help

- Heartbroken when your parent goes into a downward spiral emotionally

- Hurt that your parent doesn't spend much time with you anymore

"Sometimes I tend to carry all his (my dad's) emotions on my shoulders, in addition to all that I'm going through... deep down we love our parents, but I think it can become heavy."
Marie-Pier[3]

■ Lonely and down when your friends don't seem to understand (more on dealing with friends in Chapter 13)

How about you?

Think about a time when you felt especially sad about your parent.

Describe what was going on in your family: _____

_____

What were you thinking? _____

_____

How did you get through that time? _____

_____

During the tough times, I feel more hopeful when I remember that my parent (check all that apply):

❏ Has good friends

❏ Goes to therapy

❏ Has bounced back from hard times before

❏ Takes medication to help with their symptoms

❏ Loves me and shows it the best they can

❏ Is honest about how they're feeling rather than hiding or denying it

❏ Has a lot of strength and courage

❏ Keeps trying, even when it's hard

❏ Others: _____

_____

Hint: Especially when feeling sad, it's important to take care of yourself. Spending time with a trusted friend or distracting yourself with a hobby or exercise may ease a bit of the hurt. You may also want to explore seeing a therapist yourself, perhaps at school or in the community.

If your sadness becomes intense or lasts for over a week OR if you ever have thoughts of suicide or harming yourself, please talk to a trusted adult right away. You can contact 988 (Suicide & Crisis Lifeline) as well. Be sure to check out Chapters 11 and 16 for helpful tips on managing your own strong feelings.

Confusion

Mental illness can be hard to understand. Unlike if your parent has a broken leg that can be seen on an x-ray, many symptoms of mental illness are invisible to an outsider. It's hard to describe and understand things you cannot see.

Teenagers may struggle with questions such as:

- *Why did my stepmom stop taking her medications? She had been doing so well.*

- *Why won't my dad stop drinking and smoking pot every day? He knows they're not good for his mental health but he just won't quit.*

- *Why did my mom develop PTSD after the tornado came through our neighborhood? No one was hurt, our house wasn't damaged, and everyone else is handling it pretty well. Why is she struggling so much?*

- *Why won't my dad admit he has a problem and get help? He's so stubborn and proud, but I think professionals could really help him.*

How about you?

Think about your parent and their experience of mental illness and complete the following sentences:

I feel confused when my parent _____

_____

I wish someone would explain _____

_____

Sometimes I wonder if my parent will ever _____

_____

I don't understand why _____

_____

You may have many unanswered questions. What might you like to ask:

Your parent who has the illness? _____

_____

Your other parent/caregiver or another family member? _____

_____

A professional such as doctor or therapist? _____

_____

Hint: At the end of the day, remember that some things simply don't have easy answers. While it's important to ask questions and do the research to learn what you can from reputable sources, part of coping can be learning to live with uncertainty. It's OK to not have it all figured out.

Anger

Living with someone with a mental illness can be unpredictable. Your mom may seem in good spirits one day, but then be confused and paranoid the next—what happened? Why can't she just be like other moms? Sometimes it just doesn't feel fair. You may be tired of walking on eggshells, never knowing what might set her off.

It's normal to feel angry at times with your parent—both for what they do and don't do. There may be a lot of tension in your house. Perhaps your parents argue a lot, which can also be hard on you.

Although society says it's NOT OK to be angry, we disagree. Anger is a basic human emotion that every-body experiences. As previously mentioned, it's how you choose to act on that feeling that matters. Acting aggressively can have negative consequences, which is why this emotion can get a bad reputation.

"It made me angry not to understand what was going on ... anger towards myself, towards my mother, towards my family who didn't explain things to me."
Marianne[3]

Teens whose parent has a mental illness may feel angry toward a variety of people. For example, some feel:

angry at _____*my family*_____ because *I just want to hang out with my friends and live my own life without having to worry about them*.

angry at _____*my mom*_____ because *I don't know why she has to be like this. I feel abandoned at a time when I need her to be there for me.*

angry at _____*my friends*_____ because *they seem to have perfect lives and don't have to deal with all this stress.*

How about you?

If you've been experiencing anger recently, think about who you are angry with and why:

I'm angry with _____ for / because _____

_____ .

I'm angry with _____ for / because _____

_____ .

Hint: We'll talk about many strategies in Part 3 for dealing with strong feelings, including anger. When you are very upset, it can help to take a pause—give yourself time to settle down before reacting in a way you later regret. You may want to get away from the situation and do something you enjoy, perhaps an activity in the list on page 131.

Embarrassment

At times you may feel embarrassed by your mom or dad's behavior. You may avoid having friends over to your house because you cannot predict your parent's mood or how they might act. You may also feel disappointed, such as when your friends' parents attend the volleyball tournament but your mom or dad doesn't show up.

How about you?

Think about a time when you felt embarrassed or upset about your parent's behavior.

Please describe what happened. What was most difficult for you?

_____

_____

What were you thinking? What did you do? _____

_____

_____

Hint: In addition to acknowledging your hurt feelings and (hopefully!) seeking support for yourself, you might also try taking your parent's perspective. Perhaps you can consider that they're doing the best they can. For example, after an angry outburst in public, your parent may later feel humiliated and ashamed. They may be disappointed in themselves when they aren't well enough to support you in your activities. Now, you may absolutely still feel embarrassed, angry, or sad—and it's not your responsibility to deal with your parent's feelings—but considering that they may regret their behavior might be helpful for you.

Guilt

When you feel impatient, hurt, or annoyed with your parent, you may say or do things that you later regret. Perhaps you make fun of, ignore, or raise your voice to your mom or dad. Maybe you say unkind things about your parent to other people. You may also think about wanting to escape your situation, such as wishing they weren't your parent or that you could live somewhere else.

Later on, you may feel guilty.

Let's consider how 15-year-old Ramon feels in the following situation:

> *Ramon had a solo in his choir concert and was angry with his mom for not coming. Her excuse of "I was too tired" was just lame and disappointing. Ramon was mad and thought she was being selfish.*
>
> *However, later Ramon felt badly about himself. He thought, "I really shouldn't feel angry with Mom. She's tired because she doesn't sleep much. I know she has a lot of anxiety and sometimes has panic attacks in crowds, so the large audience at the concert would have been stressful for her anyway. Maybe I don't have a right to feel angry."*

Although Ramon feels guilty for his angry feelings, he has every right to be upset. Even though he understands that his mom's mental health problems probably contributed to her missing his concert, Ramon is experiencing disappointment and anger—totally understandable feelings in that situation, and nothing to feel guilty about.

Hint: Just like with anger, remember to separate your behavior from your thoughts and feelings about guilt.

If you act disrespectfully and later feel guilty, the emotion may be trying to tell you something. For example, if Ramon had yelled at his mom for being self-centered, he probably would have regretted it later. This kind of guilt may motivate him to make a different decision in the future, one he'll feel better about. Taking a pause between having an intense thought/feeling and acting on it can give you more self-control and often lead to a better outcome.

Anxiety

All human beings live with a certain amount of anxiety, and it can show up in your feelings, thoughts, and body. Emotionally, you may feel wound up, nervous, tense, and afraid. Perhaps you worry a lot about bad things that could happen in the future. You may experience anxiety as tightness in your chest, restlessness, sweating, or a pit in your stomach. Intense anxiety can feel overwhelming and may even escalate into a panic attack.

Anxiety can serve many helpful functions, such as keeping you alert, motivated to take action, and aware of risky situations. Like with other emotions, anxiety fluctuates over time, and difficult situations with your parent can certainly increase your stress level. Sometimes it may feel like you're carrying the weight of the world on your shoulders, which can make it hard to concentrate, relax, and sleep.

How about you?

Here is a list of worries experienced by many teenagers whose parent has a mental illness. Check those that you identify with:

- ❏ I get scared when my parent is out of control.
- ❏ I worry that my parent may never get better. What will their future be like?
- ❏ I'm afraid of opening up to others because they might distance from me or make fun of my family.
- ❏ I worry that my family will depend on me too much and that I will never be free to live my own life.
- ❏ I worry about what other people think about our family.
- ❏ I'm afraid I might develop a mental illness one day.
- ❏ Other worries you have? If so, describe them here: _____

_____

Hint: You may decide to let others know about your anxiety and worries, or you may choose to keep these feelings to yourself. It's totally your decision, but *remember that pain and fear often intensify when kept hidden inside.* Although opening up to someone may feel uncomfortable, being heard and encouraged can offer considerable relief . . . for anxiety and all of the feelings discussed in this chapter. You don't have to manage this alone.

How about you?

Think about how you manage anxiety or stress.

What helps you to feel grounded and safe when you are worried or afraid?

_____

Where do you go? _____

_____

What do you do?_____

_____

Who is reassuring and comforting? _____

_____

CHAPTER 10

How to Express Your Feelings

The Seven Cs poem highlights many of the key messages described in Part Two of this book, including that you did not cause your parent's illness and that you cannot cure or control it. Although the poem was originally written for families managing substance abuse, the messages apply to mental illness as well. In this chapter, we focus on being true to yourself and communicating your feelings.

> **The Seven Cs**
>
> You didn't Cause it.
>
> You can't Cure it.
>
> You can't Control it.
>
> You can help take Care of yourself
>
> By Communicating your feelings,
>
> Making healthy Choices,
>
> And Celebrating being yourself.
>
> National Association for Children of Alcoholics[4]

Wearing a "Mask"

At some point during the Covid-19 pandemic, nearly everyone wore a physical mask to prevent the spread of the virus. But, many of us wear a different kind of mask when we want to hide our feelings from others.

Being honest and letting people know your true feelings takes courage. Telling others what's going on at home may feel risky. You might worry about how they would respond and if they would keep it private. Perhaps you fear you could become emotional and feel awkward. Sometimes it may seem easier to just keep things to yourself.

Let's see how Miguel deals with this situation.

Miguel's mom, Anita, has schizophrenia. She uses marijuana to try to relax and block out her voices, but she actually becomes more paranoid and agitated when she smokes. Although Miguel would like to pretend her behavior doesn't bother him, he is worried. Miguel tries to act normally at school and around his friends. This works fine for a while, but eventually things spiral when Anita thinks her family is poisoning her. It's just too hard for Miguel to fake it and hide behind his mask any longer. He talks to his school counselor and appreciates her listening and support. He and his brother, Bruno, also have some honest talks, which is helpful for both of them.

How about you?

Can you think of a time when you wore a mask like Miguel did?   Yes   No

If yes, what did your mask say?_____

_____

What did your mask hide? _____

_____

Is there anyone in your life or any place you can go where you don't need a mask?

_____

Some teens wear a mask for so long that they convince themselves that they are "just fine." Some keep busy and distracted so they don't have to think about what's going on. They may even feel numb and convince themselves that their family situation doesn't affect them.

If you find yourself doing this, there's good news and bad news. The good news is that wearing a mask can sometimes work—for a little while. The pain may feel less intense in the moment, and you may be able to carry on pretending everything is fine.

However, there's some bad news about hiding or denying your feelings. Emotions stuffed inside can lead to other problems. You may:

- Become lonely and feel even worse

- Struggle to experience genuine happiness or joy

- Get sick often, such as frequent headaches or stomachaches

- Notice your feelings behind the mask boil over into other relationships

- Have strong emotional reactions that are out of proportion to the situation

- Get into trouble at school or argue with your friends and siblings more than usual

Therefore, it helps to find safe, healthy ways to express your feelings. The rest of this chapter describes three ways of taking off your mask and expressing yourself: verbally, in writing, and through art and music.

Expressing Your Feelings Verbally

There may be times when you want to talk to someone about what's going on at home, but you don't know where to start. You know you have strong feelings inside and want to speak your truth.

A few pointers about sharing personal matters:

✓ **Who?**
Picking the right person who will listen without judgment is important. More on that in Chapter 12.

✓ **What if I'm nervous?**
It's normal to feel a bit anxious when sharing from the heart. You might write a few notes before the discussion about what you plan to share. You may begin the conversation by mentioning that this is hard for you. The other person will probably respect your courage for opening up.

✓ **What if I get emotional or become overwhelmed?**
If you start to feel overwhelmed, you may want to take a few breaths to calm down. A good friend will understand your tears and be patient.

✓ **How much should I share?**
You might decide to explain a bit and see how the other person responds. Hopefully the discussion goes well and you want to continue another time. You don't have to share everything in the first conversation if you don't want to.

✓ **How can they help?**

You could also tell them how they could be supportive. For example, do you want them to ask questions? Give you a hug? Offer advice? Just listen? Distract you? Something else?

✓ **Will it be private?**

Unless someone is in danger (in which case an adult should be involved), you might ask your friend to keep what you shared private.

Although it's impossible to know for sure how someone will respond to your sharing, many teens are pleasantly surprised. The other person might know someone living with a mental illness themselves, so can relate at a personal level. However, even if they don't have the same circumstances in their family, they may be able to listen and support you far better than you'd hoped.

Chapter 13 further explores how to express your feelings verbally and focuses specifically on your friendships. It addresses what you might choose to share with your friends and how to deal with their reactions.

Expressing Your Feelings in Writing

Another excellent way of sorting through strong feelings is by writing. You may use a journal, computer, tablet, or other device. Remember that spelling, grammar, and organization don't matter! In fact, worrying too much about them can slow you down. All that matters is that you pick a private place where you won't be bothered. You may be surprised at what comes out when you start writing. When you're done, you can rip it up, delete the document, keep it for later, put it in a private place, or share it with a family member, friend, or therapist. It's totally up to you.

Some teens find it helpful to write their parent a letter to share their feelings. After you finish, you can decide whether or not to give it to them. Just start writing and see what happens.

Dear Mom/Dad:

_____

_____

_____

_____

_____

_____

_____

_____

_____

_____

If you need help getting started, these prompts may be helpful:

I want you to know that...   *Thank you for...*

It's so hard when...   *I admire you for...*

I worry that...   *I miss how our relationship used to be. I miss...*

I would like it if we could (share specifics of what you would like to do together) ...

If you decide to give your parent the letter, be prepared for a variety of possible responses. Best case scenario, it will spark honest conversation that will strengthen your relationship; your parent could honor your feelings and perhaps the two of you could commit to spending more quality time together. However, depending on the content of your letter and your parent's current well-being, it could be hard for them to read. They may need time to digest it before being ready to talk. Also, be aware that they may express sadness, hurt, or anger toward you, which could be hard to hear. Please be thoughtful about your decisions surrounding *if* and *when* to share such a personal letter.

Even if you get no response (or a painful one), remember that a large part of why you wrote the letter was for yourself—not your parent. You took the time and energy to connect with and write about your feelings. Strong work.

Expressing Your Feelings Through Art and Music

In addition to speaking and writing about your feelings, some people find art and music to be great ways of connecting with emotions and expressing them. The process can be a way of translating what you feel into something you see or hear.

If you like creative projects, you might draw, paint, make bracelets, work with clay, color, create a dream catcher, or do origami. You could even make a collage (online or with magazines) of pictures that reflect your feelings.

If you enjoy music, you can sing or play an instrument—both great ways to express your feelings. You could make a video, dance, write music, or create a playlist of songs that you relate to right now.

For both art and music, please try to enjoy the process rather than judging the outcome. Engaging with artistic activities can be relaxing and can enable you to connect with and express your feelings freely, without being confined by words.

> **The only feelings that do not heal are the ones you hide.**
> Henri Nouwen[5]

CHAPTER 11

How to Cope With the Rough Times

As we have discussed, many feelings can surface when your parent has a mental illness. Now that you have named some difficult emotions, this chapter offers concrete tools for coping.

It's normal to want to avoid pain and suffering—physical pain such as headaches or emotional pain such as depression. As explored in Chapter 10, some people wear a mask and try to pretend they aren't hurting. Others use alcohol or drugs, behave in dangerous ways, or hang out with friends who aren't a great influence. These choices can create long-term problems. They may take you down a road that isn't consistent with your values—with the kind of person you want to be.

As highlighted in Fact #6, it's important to take good care of yourself. Let's look at some healthy coping skills, some you may already be using and others you might want to consider.

Learning From the Past

> **How about you?**
>
> Let's start by thinking about a past tough situation. Maybe a difficult issue with a friend, the death of a pet, a serious physical health problem in a family member, or your parents' divorce.
>
> What was that situation?_____
>
> _____
>
> What helped you get through it?_____
>
> _____
>
> What did you learn about yourself? _____
>
> _____

As you face the challenge of your parent's mental illness, consider drawing upon what worked in the past. You've navigated difficulties before. You've been resilient by continuing to move forward even when things felt awful. Can those experiences remind you of your strength? Perhaps so, perhaps not. Just something to consider.

Coping Strategies

Now let's get specific and consider the following activities that work for many teens in managing strong feelings. Rate each activity on a scale of 1-5 according to how helpful it is (or might be) for you.

1	2	3	4	5
Not at All		Somewhat Helpful		Very Helpful

_____ Listen to music	_____ Play with your pet	_____ Write in a journal
_____ Go for a walk or run	_____ Play a musical instrument	_____ Call or text a friend
_____ Watch a movie	_____ Use a relaxation app	_____ Read a book or blog
_____ Yoga	_____ Spend time in nature	_____ Take a bath or shower
_____ Play a video game	_____ Talk to a counselor	_____ Take a nap
_____ Pray or meditate	_____ Take deep breaths	_____ Cry
_____ Volunteer	_____ What else? _____	

Different coping strategies work for different situations. How about experimenting with something new? Circle a couple of these activities that sound interesting and that you might want to try.

A few reminders about coping:

✓ What works for one person may not work for someone else—so be open to trying several options.

✓ What you choose depends on how you feel, who is around, and what you need at the time. Be flexible!

✓ Anything taken to extremes can cause problems (so this isn't a ticket to play video games all day long!).

✓ Look for the 5%! Have realistic expectations when you try something new, and you may want to give the coping tool a few tries. Feeling just 5% better can make a meaningful difference.

Let's meet three teenagers and see how they deal with their feelings and complex family situations.

Santosh

Life at home is rough for Santosh. His dad has bipolar disorder and experiences intense mood swings—which are a lot worse since he started a stressful new job. Santosh's parents argue frequently, so things feel pretty tense around the house. Because Santosh wants to avoid the family drama, he spends a lot of time at the community center. Last week Santosh got into a fight at school and then had an argument with his dad after dinner. Santosh's stress level is higher than ever.

Distracting Yourself and Having Fun

When you feel overwhelmed, getting some distance from the situation can help. Although it's not a good idea to avoid reality all the time, taking a break and distracting yourself can be healthy.

It's possible that you may feel guilty if you have fun while your parent is struggling. However, remember that it's important to set boundaries for your own well-being, and *you are not responsible for your parent's happiness.*

When Santosh wants to escape the stress at home, he likes to:

- Listen to his favorite playlist
- Play video games
- Read a book
- Play strategy board games with friends
- Watch his favorite comedy show
- Take his puppy to the dog park

How about you?

What best distracts you from the difficulties at home?_____

_____

_____

_____

_____

_____

_____

_____

Doing Something Physical

Being physically active is an excellent way to release stress and improve your well-being. When you exercise, your body releases endorphins—brain chemicals that can give you energy and lift your mood. Regular physical activity can also improve your sleep and self-esteem. Bonus points for outdoor exercise, fresh air, and sunshine!

"When you have a parent with a mental illness, it's heavy, it's tiring...you worry about them all the time. When you go for a hike in nature...it's so calming...it allows you to relax, to rest..."
Joani[3]

Santosh knows that the following activities help his mood and his ability to deal with stress:

- Lift weights

- Go for a run

- Play pick-up basketball at the community center

- Go on a bike ride

- Play tennis with his cousin

How about you?

What physical activities help you release stress? _____

_____

_____

_____

_____

_____

_____

Lucia

Lucia and her stepdad, Victor, struggle to get along. She feels on edge and confused by his unpredictable behavior. Victor is a veteran and had a couple combat tours. Although Lucia doesn't know much about that part of his life, she knows that loud noises such as thunder and fireworks are hard for him. Lucia's mom said Victor has PTSD and anxiety from both his time in the military and his job as a police officer.

A few months ago, Victor saw some kids get badly injured at a huge riot downtown when he was on patrol. Since that time, he won't let anyone in the family go to that part of town. He's overprotective—frequently texting Lucia when she's out with friends to make sure she's safe. Although Victor can be sweet, he gets triggered by seeing violence on TV and becomes agitated and mean. When that happens, Lucia retreats to her room. Her mom gets defensive when Lucia tries to share her feelings about Victor. Lucia would love to be able to talk to someone who could understand.

Expressing Your Feelings and Finding Support

As discussed in the last chapter, identifying and expressing your feelings when you feel upset can be helpful. Some days you may share your thoughts and emotions with someone else, while other times you want to process them privately.

Lucia finds it helpful to:

- Talk to her best friend's mom

- Journal in her diary

- Talk to her best friend

- Write poems or short stories

- Talk to and pray with her youth minister at church

How about you?

What works well for you in expressing your feelings? _____

_____

_____

Who can you talk openly to about your feelings? (more on your support network in the next chapter). _____

_____

_____

Helping Others

Although the idea of doing more when you are emotionally exhausted may sound ridiculous, a great coping tool is helping others. Lucia might enjoy getting away from her family stress, and it may feel good to support people or a cause she believes in.

If you're open to helping others or volunteering, consider these three ideas:

> Great opportunities to help others seldom come...
> but small ones surround us every day.
>
> Sally Koch

1. You have probably learned a lot in your journey of having a parent with a mental illness. You could help someone else in a similar situation. Keep that in mind if the opportunity arises. Given the prevalence of mental illness, it's a highly likely that you

know other kids whose parent has significant emotional problems—although it's quite possible you may not know *who* or the specifics of *what* they're experiencing.

Consider this scenario

A friend from your soccer team told you that his mom was recently diagnosed with a mental illness. He said he doesn't know a lot about mental health problems, and he feels pretty confused and overwhelmed.

What do you think would be helpful for your friend to know? _____

_____

What do you wish someone had told you? _____

_____

---

2. In thinking about how you might want to help others more broadly, ask yourself: What do I like doing? Do I enjoy spending time with animals such as at a zoo or animal shelter? Visiting the elderly, perhaps an older neighbor? Working at a food shelf? Spending time with people living with intellectual disabilities, such as with the Special Olympics? Regardless of the specific activity, volunteering can be a great way to meet people who share your interests and possibly make new friends.

Lucia's next-door neighbor recently had knee surgery. Since Lucia loves animals, she volunteered to walk his dog, which was a win-win for everyone. It got Lucia out of the house, she had fun with the dog, and it sure helped her neighbor during his recovery.

3. In addition to these traditional volunteer opportunities, begin by thinking small. Might there be something kind you could do this week? You'd be surprised what a difference a small gesture can make, and you may walk away feeling pretty good as well.

Think about the last time you did some small act of kindness. What did you do?

_____

_____

How did you feel afterwards? _____

_____

If perhaps it's been a while, what might you do in the near future? If so, describe it here:_____

_____

Kim

Kim isn't sure exactly what she's feeling but knows she's stressed about her family. Her stomach is in knots, and she struggles to sleep at night. Kim knows that her mom recently stopped taking her medications for depression. She remembers that the last time this happened her mom became very depressed and had to take a leave of absence from work. So why did she stop her meds again? Kim just doesn't get it and worries what might happen next. She would sure like to be able to relax and get a good night's sleep.

Gathering Information

When you feel confused, it can help to face the situation head on, approach it logically, and learn about the topic. Gathering facts and getting into your head can help you understand and feel less afraid. Knowledge is powerful.

You may want to be cautious about information you find online, especially from social media, as inaccurate messages can spread quickly. See the Resource List on page 133 for sources that offer information grounded in science.

Kim finds it helpful to:

- Follow reputable mental health organizations on social media

- Talk to her school counselor and godmother

- Read articles and blogs

- Talk to her dad and older brother

- Reach out to her friend, Savannah, whose mom deals with depression and anxiety. Savannah is not only a good listener, but she often has helpful advice

As Kim gathers information, she better understands what may be going on with her mom, including common reasons that people stop taking their medication. Although still quite worried, Kim feels less confused. Learning about mental illness helps her feel calmer and more able to cope.

How about you?

When you have questions about mental illness, what is your go-to source?

_____

_____

Who do you trust to answer your questions and give solid advice about mental illness? _____

_____

Relaxing and Being Kind to Yourself

Tension and stress affect not only your thoughts and feelings, but they can also show up in your body. Kim's upset stomach and sleeping problems are examples of the mind-body connection. When revved up emotionally, it can help to do something calming.

Kim learned some relaxation techniques from her counselor, including square breathing. As seen in this diagram, this skill involves slow, deep breathing to calm the nervous system. Each step lasts for 4 seconds, and you repeat it as many times as you wish. You can do this exercise anywhere, at any time. It can be especially helpful for falling asleep.

Square Breathing

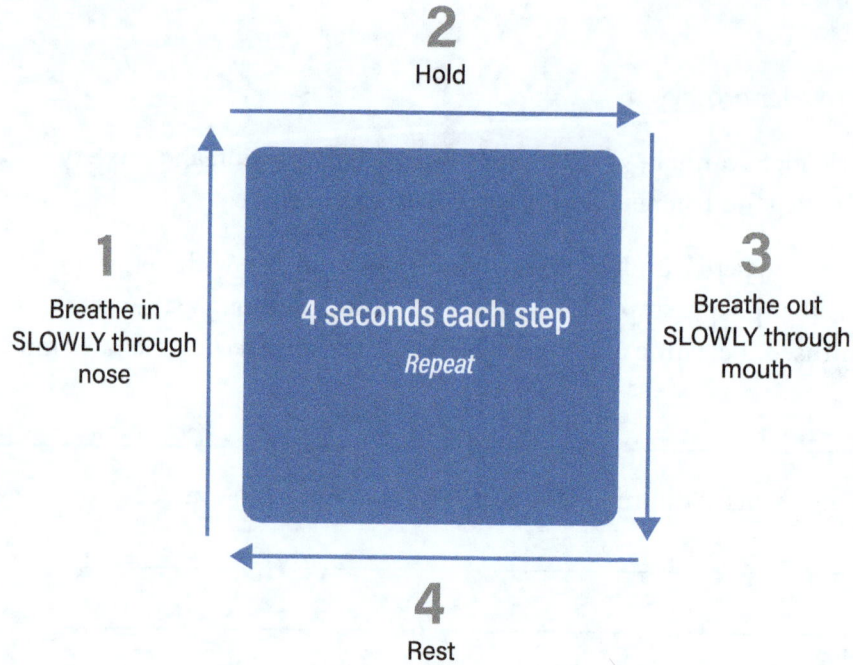

When Kim is sad or stressed, not only does she feel the tension in her body, but she's also hard on herself. She is her own worst critic. When something doesn't go perfectly, she dwells on what she did wrong and has a hard time letting it go.

Kim read and really related to a blog by psychologist Kristin Neff, PhD, which talked about **self-compassion** and how to offer yourself more kindness and grace. Kim learned how to accept situations—such as her mom's depression—for what they are rather than trying to change them. When she started to fall into the old critical spiral, she stopped and asked herself, "What would I say to a friend?" She remembered that she deserves the same kindness that she would offer someone dear to her.

When Kim wants to relax and practice self-compassion, she finds it helpful to:

- Take a long bath or shower

- Practice square breathing

- Reflect on how she would support a friend in that situation, and then offer herself the same kindness

- Stretch or do yoga

- Imagine herself walking along the ocean, feeling the sun on her face, and hearing the waves hitting the sand

- Remind herself that everybody goes through hard times…and that she will get through this difficult period

How about you?

What specific activities calm your spirit? _____

_____

Is there a place that is peaceful for you? If so, describe it:_____

_____

How might you offer yourself more kindness and grace? _____

_____

CHAPTER 12

Who You Can Count on for Support

Having a parent with a mental illness can feel lonely at times. Perhaps no one in your family talks about your parent's illness—it's the proverbial elephant in the room. Or, maybe your family does talk openly, but it feels like no one understands what it's like for you. Also, it may seem like none of your friends are dealing with anything similar. All of this can feel isolating.

Although it may be tempting to distance from other people and keep your feelings to yourself, we hope you don't make that a habit. Isolating and pushing down your emotions can make you feel worse, and your distress may show up as headaches or upset stomach. On the other hand, sharing your struggles with a trustworthy person can make things feel less overwhelming.

Figuring out who can be supportive is important. Choose people who will:

- Listen without judging or interrupting you

- Try to understand your feelings and experience

- Offer kindness and empathy

- Keep your conversations private

> Sometimes we need someone to simply be there.
>
> Not to fix or do anything in particular, but just to let us know we are supported and cared about.

This chapter focuses on two groups of people who may be able to support you: your immediate family and other people in your life.

Your Immediate Family

People in your immediate family may know you better than anyone else. Sometimes talking with one or both of your parents just feels right. At other times, you might open up to a sibling, and you can support each other. Or, perhaps you want to distract yourself from all the stress, so you hang out with a younger brother or sister who loves your attention.

If you have another parent or caregiver in the house, they can easily become overwhelmed or burned out. Supporting a spouse/partner with a mental illness can take a lot of time and energy—oftentimes going to appointments, communicating with doctors, advocating with insurance companies, managing the bills, dealing with challenging behavior and crises, and so on. Some partners get a second job to bring in extra income to cover the expenses. It can be a lot.

When both parents are stretched thin, they may not have as much time and energy as usual to support the kids. You probably sense your parents' stress. Although you may fear burdening them with your feelings or needs, most likely they DO want to hear how you're doing! With all that's going on at home, it's important to have other people who can support you as well.

Other People in Your Life

Let's look at your support network by creating a map:

1. Write **your name** in the middle.

2. In the **inner circle,** write the names of people you trust and feel connected to today. These people can be of any age. They could live nearby or across the country. You could see them every day or just occasionally. None of that matters.

Consider these people for your circles:

Parents	Aunts / uncles
Siblings	Cousins
Grandparents	A friend's parent
Friends	School counselors
Therapists	Neighbors
Teachers	Religious leaders
Youth group leaders	Coaches

Pets (not people, but super important!)

What's important is that you are comfortable talking to them about your thoughts and feelings.

3. In the **outer circle,** write the names of people who care about you, but you don't know as well. You may choose to open up to them in the future.

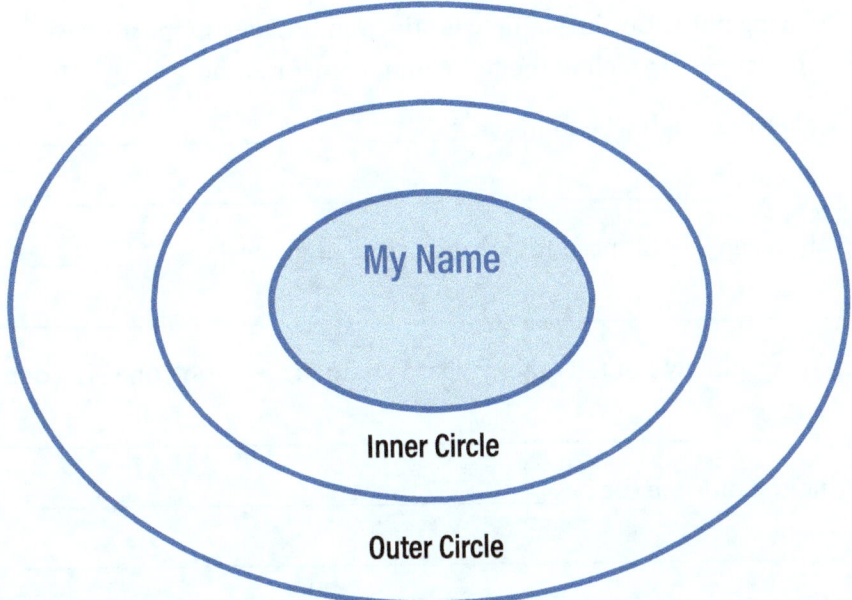

What did you notice in mapping your support network? _____

_____

_____

Did you identify anyone you might want to reach out to? _____

_____

_____

Remember that none of these people are mind readers. Although they may sense that you are struggling, they might not say anything. Perhaps they don't know what to say. Maybe they fear upsetting you or want to respect your privacy. Therefore, when you want support, it's up to you to ask for it. People are usually grateful for the opportunity to help.

Specific People for Specific Situations

Now that we've identified people in your support network, let's look at some specific situations. You probably choose different people to talk to depending on what you need at the time.

How about you?

Considering both your immediate family and broader support network, write in names of people for each of the following. Someone who:

Makes me laugh when I'm sad _____

_____

Will listen when I need to talk, any time night or day _____

_____

Will absolutely not tell others what I share (unless someone is in danger)

_____

Understands me the best_____

_____

Will be there when I need to cry_____

_____

Can drive me to activities when I need a ride_____

_____

Will help me if I ever feel in danger _____

_____

Can support me at school _____

_____

Note: If you struggle to identify people for these situations, please be gentle with yourself. Making and maintaining friendships can be hard. If you are able to list one person who is a true friend, you are lucky indeed. Also, don't forget the support and unconditional love that pets can offer!

CHAPTER 13

What to Tell Your Friends and How to Fight Stigma

For many teenagers, how you're viewed by peers feels pretty important. Perhaps you wonder if people judge you for the clothes you wear, your grades, your athletic ability, or the friends you keep. While you have control over some of these things, many you do not. Having a parent with a mental illness is one of those things you simply cannot control.

The reality is that all families have difficulties, be it physical health problems, divorce, money problems, alcohol or drug abuse, legal problems, or family violence. If you could look behind the doors of every house on your block, you would see that *every family is struggling with something.*

One of the challenges your family manages is your parent's illness—which can be tricky to explain. This chapter considers how you talk with your friends about mental illness, and how to fight the stigma surrounding it.

Should You Open Up to a Friend?

You may have gotten strong messages from one or both of your parents about discussing the mental illness outside of your household. Some families encourage open discussion, and they share freely with friends, relatives, and healthcare professionals. Other families work hard to keep the illness a secret, which can make matters tougher . . . teens can feel pretty lonely and confused.

Although being thoughtful about your parents' wishes is important, ultimately you make the decisions about **who you tell** and **what you tell them**. If your parents insist on privacy, you might ask to see a therapist, perhaps even a counselor or social worker at school.

In making decisions about what to say and to whom, you may create a Pros and Cons list such as Jamila does.

> *Jamila's dad has major depression which has gotten a lot worse since he hurt his back in an ATV accident. He became dependent on the narcotic medications prescribed for the pain, and it developed into an addiction to opioids. It's heartbreaking for Jamila when her dad is hurting so much—both physically and emotionally. Jamila made the following lists:*

Pros of Telling My Friends	Cons of Telling My Friends
Maybe they could be supportive and helpful	They might not get it at all
I wouldn't have to keep things bottled up inside any longer	I'd feel nervous telling them
They might know someone else who has depression or an addiction so could relate	They may be uncomfortable and just change the subject. That could feel even worse
They'd understand why my dad doesn't always attend my school events	They may think my dad is "crazy" and weak
Sharing about my dad might help decrease stigma about mental illness and addiction. It's OK to talk about it. It's nothing to be ashamed of!	They may treat my dad (or me) differently
	Their parents may not let them come to my house out of fear of his behavior
	They might tell other people
	My dad may feel betrayed and angry if I share this personal information

For Jamila, seeing these lists on paper helped her sort through her mixed feelings—both her hopes and her fears about sharing with her friends.

What would a Pros and Cons list look like for you? Consider filling in this table with possible benefits and risks of sharing with your friends about your parent's illness:

Pros of Telling My Friends	Cons of Telling My Friends

What Might You Tell Your Friends?

In addition to deciding *if* you want to open up to your friends, it's helpful to think about *what* to tell them. Your friends certainly know about mental illness, but they probably don't know what it's like to live with someone managing it—unless someone in their family is experiencing it as well.

If you confide in your friends, you may decide to take it gradually. Perhaps you share some information, see how they respond, and then decide if you want to continue. If you're not sure what to say or where to start, consider drawing from the facts from Chapter 1. You might also share some of these messages:

- *My family is not alone. About half of all people have a mental illness at some point in their lives.*

- *At any given time, about 1 in 5 teenagers has a parent with a mental illness.*

- *My parent has a serious mental illness (schizophrenia / bipolar disorder / depression), something that affects about 1 in 20 people during their lifetime.*

- *My parent has posttraumatic stress disorder or PTSD from her combat experiences in the military. There are many helpful treatments for PTSD, and she gets a lot of support from other veterans at the Vet Center.*

- *Many people with a mental illness recover. Their symptoms become less intense, and/or they learn how to manage them well. Even during hard times, I hold onto hope.*

- *Managing a mental illness takes a lot of work. I'm proud of my parent for working hard on feeling better.*

- *My parent has found a lot of help from his friends at the clubhouse as well as his therapist and psychiatrist. I'm glad he has so much support.*

Dealing With Friends' Reactions

If you decide to open up to your friends about your parent's illness, be prepared for a variety of reactions. It can be hard to predict how someone will respond. People may surprise you, perhaps by being more understanding and supportive than you anticipated. Being truly heard feels good, and you may walk away feeling grateful and lighter.

> True friends aren't the ones who make your problems disappear.
>
> They are the ones who won't disappear when you are facing problems.

On the other hand, some conversations may be awkward and upsetting; people may not know what to say or how to be helpful. If you are dismissed or judged after sharing, please take care of yourself. Try reaching out to someone you identified in Chapter 12 or consider journaling about your hurt and angry feelings. Bottom line: you deserve to have kind, encouraging people go through this journey with you, and you can set boundaries or walk away from those that are not supportive.

How about you?

Have you told your good friends about your parent's mental illness? Yes No

If yes, what did you share? _____

_____

Describe a time when a friend was helpful. Maybe you felt genuinely understood or cared about. What was that like? _____

_____

Have you ever had a friend say unkind or disrespectful things—or perhaps distance from you after you shared? If so, how did you feel? What did you say or do? _____

_____

One of the reasons that people may respond in a hurtful way is because of the inaccurate information and judgmental messages they have heard about mental illness. To explore this further, let's look at the concepts of stigma and discrimination.

Stigma and Discrimination Around Mental Illness

Stigma refers to negative, judgmental attitudes or beliefs about a specific group of people. In the context of mental illness, it can refer to not only negative views of people with emotional problems, but also judgmental beliefs about seeking treatment.

Many factors affect how people view mental illness, including cultural beliefs, media portrayals, level of understanding of mental illness, personal experience of emotional problems, and relationships with people managing mental health problems.

Stigma

Negative, judgmental attitudes or beliefs

Discrimination

Unfair treatment due to the issue or illness

Stigma can show up in many ways. **Public stigma** refers to individuals judging or avoiding people with a mental illness. Fortunately, society is becoming more educated about mental illness, and some attitudes are improving. For example, recent large-scale research found that attitudes toward depression in the general public have become less stigmatizing over the past two decades. In addition, anti-stigma campaigns are attempting to raise awareness and make it OK to seek help. Some high-ranking military leaders are sharing their experiences of going to counseling for their PTSD and other mental health problems. The Department of Veterans Affairs also led a public awareness campaign with the message that "It takes the courage and strength of a warrior to ask for help." Many celebrities are openly sharing their struggles with emotional problems and their positive experiences with therapy. While progress is being made, we've still got a long way to go.

Another type of stigma involves the person feeling ashamed or guilty for having the illness, which is termed **self-stigma.** Holding such a negative view of oneself can worsen depression, increase isolation, and be a barrier to seeking help.

People living with a mental illness can also encounter **discrimination**, which is unfair treatment due to their illness. It can be subtle or obvious and may affect many aspects of life. For example, people may be discriminated against in the workplace when they are passed over for jobs, forced to take a medical leave, or fired inappropriately. They may be denied access to housing. They may experience ridicule, bullying, and harassment.

Let's further explore stigma by going back to Jamila and her family:

> *Jamila's family went through a hard time when her mom was diagnosed with advanced breast cancer. During the many months of treatment, lots of relatives, friends, and neighbors really showed up; they set up a food train for people to drop off meals, took care of Jamila's little sister, and even paid for someone to clean the house (which was awesome so Jamila didn't have to). The support of the community was amazing.*

> *A few years later, Jamila's dad went into another dark depression. His back pain flared, he quit going to work, and he talked about wanting to end his life. When things weren't getting any better, he was admitted to the hospital for a week. The staff adjusted his medication and talked about a new treatment approach for his opioid addiction.*

> *Jamila was worried about her dad. Although friends and neighbors knew what was going on, no one acknowledged it—which made the whole situation worse. No meals dropped off, no cards, and even more chores because Mom was busy with Dad at the hospital. It was sooooo hard.*

Although the lack of support from family and friends surrounding her dad's hospitalization could have been affected by many factors, stigma was probably one of them.

What Can You Do?

Stigma and discrimination surrounding mental illness are serious social issues, and many organizations and researchers are working hard to combat them. Just like with raising awareness and challenging negative attitudes about other issues that are important to you, there's a lot you can do in your everyday life about this topic.

Consider the following ways that teenagers can fight stigma and discrimination around mental illness:

Consider sharing your experience when it feels right.
What, when, with whom... your call.

Check yourself for judgmental attitudes or biases.
They can creep out in your words and actions.

Talk about it!
The more we bring the topic of mental illness out in the open, the more people will feel comfortable talking about it.

Be aware of your language.
Avoid words like crazy, psycho, or mental.

Show compassion for people who are hurting emotionally.
Remind them they're not alone, and encourage them to seek help.

Get involved!

Many organizations are actively working to combat the stigma and discrimination around mental illness. Your school may have a club or group. If not, maybe you could create a chapter yourself.

These are some groups doing great work with youth:

- Active Minds
- Bring Change to Mind
- Jed Foundation
- National Alliance on Mental Illness
- Trevor Project for LGBTQ young people

Use "people-first language."

Instead of referring to someone by their diagnosis (such as "he's schizophrenic" or "they're bipolar"), use phrases such as "has schizophrenia" or "living with bipolar disorder."

Speak up.

Give feedback when you encounter stigmatizing messages on social media or in everyday conversation.

Former First Lady Michelle Obama said it well: "Whether an illness affects your heart, your arm, or your brain, it's still an illness, and there shouldn't be any distinction. We would never tell someone with a broken leg that they should stop wallowing and get it together. We don't consider taking medication for an ear infection something to be ashamed of. We shouldn't treat mental health conditions any differently. Instead, we should make it clear that getting help isn't a sign of weakness—it's a sign of strength."[6]

CHAPTER 14

How to Strengthen Your Relationship With Your Parent

Let's now turn to what may be the most important topic in this book—namely, your relationship with your parent. Beyond your parent's experience of mental illness and its ripple effects on your family, they're first and foremost your mom or dad. Your reading this book demonstrates your desire to understand them and work on your relationship.

We'll start this chapter by considering common ways teenagers respond to their parent's illness, and then will introduce the concept of acceptance. Finally, we will explore specific strategies that might strengthen your relationship with your parent, including offering them grace.

Considering Your Role in the Family

Teens can respond in a variety of ways to having a parent struggle with a mental illness. Here are three roles that young people often play in the family:

Caregiver

Some teenagers, such as Cheyenne, are actively involved in caregiving and other family responsibilities:

> *Cheyenne, a high school sophomore, is sad and worried about her mom who was recently hospitalized due to her schizophrenia. Cheyenne's grandma stepped in and helped a lot during that time because life at home was pretty overwhelming. Cheyenne also quit the soccer team so she could come home right after school to help her younger*

sisters and prepare dinner for the family. Now that Mom is home, Cheyenne tries to lift her spirits and shares funny videos. Cheyenne double checks the pill organizer each week to make sure it's accurate, including the new medications prescribed at the hospital. Although Cheyenne misses soccer and hanging out with friends after school, nothing is as important as helping her mom.

If you relate to Cheyenne, you may be actively involved in caregiving, a role that can be meaningful but also stressful and exhausting. You might feel like you're being a parent to your parent. Facts #6 and 7 are good reminders: Although it's great to support your mom or dad, it's important to continue your own activities as well. Your well-being and relationship with your parent can be stronger when you prioritize time for yourself.

Like Cheyenne, you may help take care of your younger siblings. Your relationship with your healthier parent can also change, and somedays you may feel more like their friend than their child. Being a caregiver can stir up a lot of emotions. You may feel good about helping your family but also resent the responsibility and burden. It's important to stay connected to your own support system and make time to relax and have fun as you are able.

"When my father became ill, the line between my parents and me became blurred. I alternated between the role of parent and child…."
Daniel[3]

Comedian

Teenagers like Bernardo cope by joking around and using humor to lessen the tension at home:

Bernardo tends to avoid serious issues altogether, including his dad's depression. Bernardo has a great sense of humor and uses it to distract his family from the heaviness of what's going on. He's quite tuned in to how others are feeling and can sometimes even get his dad to laugh. Inside, however, Bernardo is worried, and feels responsible for keeping things upbeat at home. He's very uncomfortable when difficult discussions need to occur.

If you're like Bernardo, then remember Fact #7. Although humor can be healthy and it's great to support your family members, you are not responsible for their happiness. It's just not your burden to carry.

Distancer

Some teens such as Jessica distance from the family, possibly to avoid the drama at home or because they feel forgotten:

> *Everyone in Jessica's household is focused on her dad due to his recent flare-up of bipolar disorder. Her parents argue a lot. Although she's stressed about next week's calculus test and has no idea what she is going to do after graduation, she hesitates to bother her parents with her feelings and needs. She hangs out a lot at her girlfriend's house where things are a lot calmer. When she is at home, she feels invisible so stays in her room, watching videos and listening to music.*

If you see yourself in Jessica, please review Chapter 12 where you identified people who can listen and support you, especially when your parents are unable to do so. In Jessica's situation, hopefully things settle down at home, and she can reconnect with one or both of her parents… perhaps give them another try.

How about you?

Thinking about Cheyenne, Bernardo, and Jessica, do you see yourself in any of them? Yes No

If yes, what specifically are you doing as a caregiver, comedian, and/or distancer? _____

_____

Can playing that role(s) be difficult? _____

_____

If something is not working well, what might you want to change—perhaps one small thing you could do (or not do) today? _____

_____

Acknowledging the Loss and Considering Acceptance

Regardless of how you respond to your parent's mental health problems, one thing is clear: your relationship is not the same as it would be if they didn't have the illness. Having a parent struggle with a mental illness can be a kind of loss. For example, you might:

- Feel disappointed that you don't feel close to your parent

- Want your parent's advice or comfort but don't want to burden them…worrying they couldn't handle your problems with all they're managing already

- Be sad that you cannot count on them to consistently show up for you and your activities

- Wish your parent was able to deal with the everyday stresses of life without blowing up in anger

- Never know what kind of mood your parent will be in when you get home from school—that unpredictability can be hard

- Worry about the future and perhaps your responsibility for taking care of your parent someday

- Feel jealous when you see other kids with what appear to be great relationships with their parents

Recognizing this situation as a loss—a form of grief—can be sad but can also be a step toward understanding. It can free you from trying to make your parent into someone they are not. With time, you may be able to move into a mindset of **acceptance** regarding your parent's illness and your relationship with them. Acceptance doesn't mean that you necessarily like or fully understand what's going on—but that you accept "it is what it is." It involves *acknowledging and honoring the difficulties, and giving up trying to change things beyond your control.* It's absolutely not giving up hope nor accepting unkind behavior…but realizing that your parent is managing a serious illness.

Acceptance is rarely a one-time event. It may be a choice you make again and again. It's also not "all or nothing," as some things may be easier to accept than others. Acceptance can help you focus on what you have control over, rather than spending a lot of time wishing your parent or relationship were somehow different.

Giving Your Parent Grace

Along with a mindset of acceptance comes the opportunity to offer your parent grace. Although the term **grace** can be used in a religious or spiritual sense, it has much broader meanings. Offering grace can be showing kindness, love, or forgiveness when someone hurts or disappoints you. It does not mean that you don't get upset, but that you choose to respond in a polite manner.

When your parent does something that upsets you, you can pause and decide *if* and *how* to respond. Instead of automatically reacting in anger, you might try to remain calm and look at the situation differently. Perhaps you decide to let the issue go, take a break, and/or approach your parent later using words and a tone of voice that reflect respect rather than judgment.

You may find it easier to offer your parent grace when you keep the following points in mind:

- *My parent is behaving this way because they have an illness.*

- *Although I'd like to talk back to my parent right now, I'm going to take the high road and choose kindness.*

- *It must be really hard for my parent to feel so upset and overwhelmed.*

- *Even though some days it may not look like it, I know my parent is doing their best in a very difficult situation.*

- *My parent has a lot of courage and strength in managing their illness and rebuilding their life after trauma. I know it's going to take some time.*

- *Although I can't stand how my parent is acting right now, I still love and care about them.*

Now let's face it, offering someone grace can be hard! You definitely won't be able to do it every time. But we encourage you to give it a try.

Importantly, acceptance and extending grace do not mean tolerating abusive behavior of any kind. Violence (or threats thereof) and emotional abuse are never acceptable, and you should not offer grace in these situations. You deserve to be safe and consistently treated with kindness and respect (more on dealing with your parent's anger in the next chapter).

Strengthening Your Relationship With Your Parent

Although it may be easy to dwell on the hard parts of your relationship with your parent, focusing on what you admire or enjoy about them is very important. Mental illness is just one part of your parent—it does not define them or your relationship.

How about you?

How do you show your parent that you care about them (be specific)?

_____

_____

How do they usually respond? _____

_____

_____

One of the ways you can strengthen your relationship is to express your care in words—perhaps a heartfelt talk, text, email, card, meme, or even a sticky note! Consider sharing the following thoughts with your parent if and when it feels right. They would probably enjoy hearing it more than you know.

See if any of these messages might work for you:

One of my favorite things to do together is…

It's great to see you doing/enjoying…

It was so much fun when we…

Even when things are hard, I see that you keep trying. I know that you…

I love hearing you talk about…

Note: In addition to thinking through what you might want to say, be careful to avoid unkind messages, such as telling your parent to "just get over it," to "stop feeling sorry for themselves," or to "just try harder." Although these thoughts might arise, saying these words can hurt your parent and your relationship.

Beyond telling your parent how much you care, you can strengthen your relationship by simply spending time together. Although sometimes you may discuss serious issues, it's largely just being in the same space that matters. You could be doing homework and your parent might be reading, but you're together...and perhaps you take a study break to make popcorn or share a funny video.

How about you?

Here are some additional ideas. Not every idea will fit your relationship with your parent, but check out these activities you could do together:

Go on a walk or hike	Look through pictures or videos
Cook	Wash the car
Watch a sporting event	Go thrifting
Hang out at the coffee shop	Talk about fun family vacations
Get a manicure/pedicure	Go shopping
Play cards or board games	Binge watch a tv series together

What else do you enjoy doing with your parent? _____

_____

Although spending time together can be great, it's important to remember that, at times, everyone needs space. Your parent may just need to be alone. So, in addition to expressing care and hanging out together, giving your parent down time can also be kind.

CHAPTER 15

How to Cope With Crises

Sometimes life is going well without any big ups or downs. Things feel pretty stable at home, and you're not overly worried about your parent and their well-being. Then, your parent's mood or behavior change dramatically. Maybe you have seen this shift before, or perhaps it is all new. You may have sensed something was brewing, or possibly it came out of the blue. Regardless, mental health crises can be scary and confusing for everyone involved.

Let's look at some difficult situations that can happen in families managing a mental illness, such as when your parent:

- Becomes extremely angry

- Gets very depressed

- Talks about suicide

- Is admitted to the hospital

For each of the following, reflect on your family's experiences. (If the situation doesn't apply, feel free to skip it . . . or you may decide to read it so you can be prepared if it happens in the future).

Note: Throughout this chapter, we encourage you to reach out to trusted adults or crisis hotlines if you're concerned about issues of safety. We recognize that telling people outside of your family may feel risky, and you may worry about the consequences, such as the involvement of child protective services. This is an extremely difficult situation, and we honor your desire to protect your parent. However, it's important to get help when your mom or dad behaves in frightening ways. You don't have to deal with these emergency situations alone, and professionals can help your parent navigate the crisis and hopefully get back to feeling better.

Your Parent Becomes Extremely Angry

Some days your parent may be very angry, and you have no idea why. They yell or swear for no clear reason. Maybe they are irritable and react strongly to the littlest things so you walk on eggshells, trying to avoid triggering them. If your parent has an explosive temper, you might feel on edge, frightened, and angry yourself.

How about you?

Which of the following words describe your parent's anger? Check all that apply.

❑ Aggressive

❑ Argumentative

❑ Cold

❑ Condescending

❑ Intense and scary

❑ Loud

❑ Mean-spirited

❑ Out of control

❑ Punishing with the silent treatment

❑ Sarcastic

❑ Unpredictable

❑ Other: _____

Think about how you feel when your parent is angry and complete the following sentences:

I can't stand it when my parent _____

I feel scared when my parent _____

When this happens, I know that it's best for me to _____

_____

When this happens, I know I can reach out to _____

_____

Having a mental illness or history of trauma does not excuse unkind or abusive behavior. Regardless of your parent's mental health, it's never OK for them to hurt another person, especially you and your siblings. *If your parent speaks or acts in a hurtful way, STEER CLEAR as much as possible and take care of yourself.* Calling a friend, reading a book, journaling, or going for a run may help you to feel more grounded in the moment. *If you ever feel in danger, leave the situation immediately and talk to an adult or call 911.* No matter what, you deserve to feel safe and respected at home.

Importantly, most people with a mental illness are not physically aggressive. However, when under extreme stress, they may threaten others or act in a violent way. The risk of this kind of behavior is higher if they are abusing alcohol or drugs.

Your Parent Gets Very Depressed

Some people living with a mental illness go through times of serious depression which can include feeling very sad, withdrawing from others, irritability, and changes in sleep. People may have a hard time keeping up with routines like taking a shower/bath or cleaning the house.

It may be hard to understand why your parent is so depressed. You may wonder if you did something to cause them to be so withdrawn. If you look closely, you'll probably see that your parent is not only cut off from you, but they have distanced from other people and activities they used to enjoy as well.

"My dad is pretty cool, but when he's depressed, he finds it hard to do anything. He doesn't talk much or have any energy. It's like he's kind of not there when he's having a bad day."
Ben[3]

How about you?

When my parent experiences a period of dark depression, the biggest changes I see are _____

_____

When that happens, I feel _____

It helps me to_____

Sometimes my parent is physically around but just seems checked out from our family. It's like they're here—but not here. When this happens, I feel

_____

Your Parent Talks About Suicide

Suicide is a heavy topic for sure—and one that can be hard to think about. But, it's important to address because it's a leading cause of death around the world and rates are higher among people managing mental health problems. Having someone you love talk about suicide or harming themselves is frightening.

Why Do People Consider Suicide?

This is a complicated question with many possible answers. People may think about suicide when they:

- Experience so much intense emotional pain that they want to escape their life and end the hurt

- Feel very alone and sense that no one cares

- Struggle with big life challenges such as marital/relationship problems, grief, trauma, physical health problems including chronic pain, or financial problems

- Abuse alcohol or drugs—both of which can affect mood and decision making

- Feel hopeless, sensing things will never get better

- Feel like they are a burden to other people

It's important to recognize that each person's situation is unique. People who are suicidal often struggle with multiple overwhelming situations. Families and friends often wonder why their loved one considers suicide or harms themselves. The truth is that sometimes there are no clear-cut answers to these hard questions.

What Can You Do if Your Parent Talks About Suicide?

Tell a trusted adult immediately. Hearing your parent talk about wanting to die can be frightening, and you may feel helpless. Please ask someone you trust for support. Issues surrounding suicide are just too heavy and complicated to manage on your own.

Call or text 988, **the Suicide & Crisis Lifeline**. This free, confidential service is available 24/7. You can also chat on their website: https://988lifeline.org/ When you call, a trained counselor will listen, ask questions, and help you cope with the situation.

Don't keep it a secret! If your parent pressures you to keep their suicidal comments private, it's still important to tell a trusted adult. It's OK to disregard your parent's request in order to help keep them safe.

If in doubt, take it seriously and reach out. Sometimes people don't know how to communicate their emotional pain. They may not want to die, but they talk about suicide or try to harm themselves as a "cry for help." If this happens in your family, you may wonder if your parent is just trying to get attention. However, because of the potential danger involved, take all comments about suicide seriously.

Your Parent Is Admitted to the Hospital

Some people managing a mental illness go through difficult periods and need intensive support. Your parent's symptoms may be so severe that they cannot keep up their daily routines. Or, as discussed in the preceding section, perhaps they think about hurting themselves. Maybe your parent has stopped their medications or therapies, or has started drinking more or using drugs. When crises arise, a brief stay in the hospital can be beneficial.

During a hospitalization, a team of specialists works together to help your parent, often including doctors, therapists, nurses, social workers, and peer support specialists (people living with mental illness who have specialized training in helping others). The doctor may adjust your parent's medications. Your parent may participate in individual, family, or group therapy to learn how to better cope with their illness. Usually hospital stays are quite short, and the goal is to get your parent stabilized and home as soon as possible. Often the treatment team recommends additional services that could help your parent continue to recover in the weeks and months that follow.

"When she [my mom] was hospitalized, I always felt a sense of relief knowing she was safe and was being taken care of."
Guillaume[3]

For you and perhaps your siblings, this time apart from your parent can be hard. Your other parent may spend time at the hospital, leaving you alone to take care of yourselves. You may feel lonely and miss your parent. At the same time, you may feel relieved knowing your parent is getting help and you enjoy the peace at home.

Some hospital units encourage teens to visit their parents, while other units don't allow it. If the rules permit youth to visit, it's important to decide if you *want* to go. Visiting a parent in a mental health unit can be difficult. You may be happy to be with your parent, but seeing them in that setting can be sad and uncomfortable. You may notice that the unit is locked, a common practice to help keep patients safe. If you have questions or want to process your experience, talk with your other parent or possibly a nurse or social worker on the unit.

How about you?

If you visited your parent in the hospital, please describe that experience:

What was it like to see your parent in that setting? _____

_____

How did you feel? _____

_____

Did you get to talk to a nurse, doctor, or therapist? If so, how did that go?

_____

If the visit was hard for you, what did you do to take care of yourself afterwards? _____

_____

Note: It's common to feel worried and sad during times of family crisis. It may be especially important to draw upon your coping skills and support network. At the same time, crises can result in a change in your parent's treatment plan—perhaps new medications or therapies that could help them feel happier and more stable than before.

PART FOUR

Taking Care of Your Own Mental Health

CHAPTER 16

Managing Your Risk of Developing a Mental Illness and Building Resilience

Watching your parent struggle with their mental health may raise questions about your own well-being, such as…

Will I be like my parent someday?

What is my risk for developing a mental illness?

What can I do to prevent emotional problems?

As discussed in Chapter 4, mental illness is usually caused by a combination of biological factors, life experiences, and social factors. Whether or not you develop a mental illness is hard to predict. Your risk may be higher because of the genes you inherited from your parents; however, this does *not* necessarily mean you will develop an illness.

Focus on What You Can Control

Human beings tend to spend a lot of time worrying about things beyond their control. Stephen Covey, author of *Seven Habits of Highly Effective People*[7], created a model that challenges us to think about what we can control and how to be intentional about our time and energy. His concept consists of three concentric circles, namely the Circles of Concern, Influence, and Control.

The **Circle of Concern** involves matters that you care about, but actually have little ability to change. For example, you cannot control the outcome of this weekend's football game, the traffic jam that makes you late for school, or the weather for prom. Similarly, you have no control over the fact your parent has a mental illness or the side effects of their mental health medications. As discussed in Chapter 14, choosing a mindset of acceptance can be a good strategy for issues in this circle.

Things in the **Circle of Influence** are matters you can impact but ultimately don't have complete control over. Topics such as your relationships with others, how other people view you, and your physical and mental health fall in this category. It helps to devote time and energy to these issues but be realistic about your expectations.

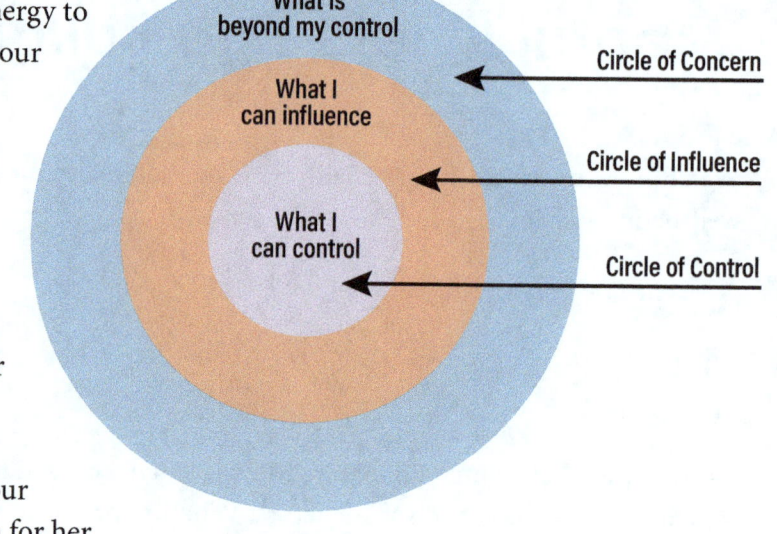

The innermost layer, the **Circle of Control**, is what you can directly impact; it includes your words, actions, attitude, and reactions to stressful situations. It may be how many hours you spend studying for the algebra test, how you respond when your friend reaches out for support, and your attitude when your grandma asks you to mow the lawn for her.

Let's apply this Circle of Control concept to your emotional well-being.

What is in Your Circle of Control With Respect to Your Mental Health?

What Can You Do to Manage Your Risk of Developing an Illness and Build Your Personal Resilience?

You obviously cannot change your genes or your past, but there is a lot you can do that affects your risk of developing a mental illness. Although you may worry about factors in the Circles of Concern and Influence, you can make the biggest impact in your Circle of Control. Consider the following five suggestions.

1. Learn About Mental Illness

Reading this book and other trustworthy sources is a great investment in your well-being. The Resource List on page 133 includes many helpful organizations, books, and hotlines for crisis situations.

Please be careful about what you read online, especially on social media. Although there are many excellent sources, some information is simply inaccurate. If you aren't sure if something is trustworthy, look at the qualifications of the author. See if they have formal training, are affiliated with a university or respected company, or are offering perspectives based on their lived experience with a mental illness. It can also be helpful to look for common themes and messages; if something just doesn't seem right, check it out on other sources or ask someone you trust. You might also look at a fact-checking resource such as snopes.com.

2. Be Aware of Warning Signs, but Don't Overinterpret Everyday Feelings

Did you know that about half of all mental health problems emerge by age 18? It's true. More serious mental illnesses (schizophrenia, major depression, and bipolar disorder) tend to develop when people are in their mid-20s or early 30s, but signs may begin to appear in adolescence. Thus, the teenage years and early adulthood are times of overall increased risk, regardless of a family history of mental illness.

One of the best things you can do is to learn about possible warning signs of mental illness. Although a complete list is beyond the scope of this book and each person's experience is different, common changes to be aware of in yourself include:

- Isolating or withdrawing from friends, family, or activities

- Sleeping a lot more or a lot less

- Changes in eating habits

- Difficulty concentrating

- Having a lot more or less energy than usual

- Feeling depressed or worrying more than usual

- Drop in grades

- Turning to or increasing your use of alcohol or drugs

Warning signs that indicate the need for **immediate** professional help include:

- Thinking seriously about suicide or hurting yourself in any way

- Thinking seriously about or planning to hurt others

- Hearing voices or seeing things that are not actually there

If you experience any of these, please tell an adult immediately. You can also call or text the 24-hour Suicide & Crisis Lifeline (988) or chat via their website (988lifeline.org). This service is free and confidential, and the trained counselor can listen, offer support, and connect you with local resources.

Although being aware of warning signs is important, *please be careful to not overinterpret everyday situations and feelings.* Most people feel sad after a relationship breakup. Moving and adjusting to a new school usually provokes anxiety. Even without specific triggers, everyone has down days when they feel lonely, tense, or discouraged. Remember that experiencing painful feelings doesn't necessarily mean you have a mental illness. It's important to notice changes from your regular feelings/thoughts/behavior that last more than a few days, cause you distress, interfere with your regular routines, or don't improve with your current coping strategies. If you are struggling, please talk to someone you trust, perhaps someone you identified in Chapter 12.

3. Seek Help Early

Approximately 1 in 5 teens in the general population experiences an episode of depression by age 18, and about 1 in 3 deals with considerable anxiety. So, if you're struggling, you're definitely not alone.

Research is clear: it's better to see a mental health professional sooner rather than later. It's easier for professionals to help when problems first emerge rather than in the midst of a crisis. Although there is no lab test that can definitively predict or diagnose an emerging illness, healthcare providers can monitor your well-being and be on the lookout for more serious difficulties.

Early intervention may also help prevent a full-blown illness from developing. Sadly, only half of youth with mental health problems receive treatment, due in part to stigma and the many barriers to getting care discussed in Chapter 8. We hope you can be in that 50% that does get help. If the first thing you try doesn't work out, speak up and try something else.

4. Make Healthy Lifestyle Choices

While adults often tell teens to do stuff because "it's good for you," adolescence is a time of making your own decisions about lots of things, including issues that affect your health. In this section, we focus on the lifestyle choices that can make the biggest impact on your well-being.

You've no doubt heard the following recommendations before—but did you know that these behaviors can significantly impact both your physical and mental health? Interestingly, research in the general population has found that some of these habits can reduce the risk for *developing* mental health problems in the first place. And, all of them can help people managing depression or anxiety to feel better.

Be Physically Active (and remember strength training, too)

✓ You don't have to run a marathon. It's just important to move your body so that your heart rate goes up. Although national guidelines recommend one hour of moderate to vigorous physical activity most days, just 30 minutes, three days per week, can make a big difference.

✓ Alternate aerobic exercise with strength training. Do a few reps with dumbbells or exercise bands, consider sit-ups or squats, or try yoga to build your strength (of course, talk to your doctor about what is safe for you).

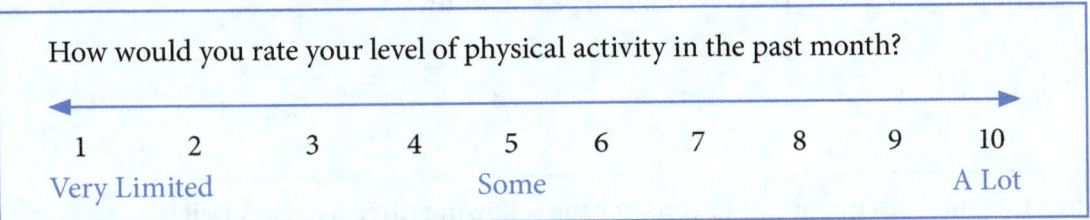

How would you rate your level of physical activity in the past month?

1	2	3	4	5	6	7	8	9	10
Very Limited				Some					A Lot

Eat a Healthy Diet

✓ Strive to make healthy choices, including a lot of fruits, vegetables, fish, and whole grain products.

✓ Work to have healthy eating habits, including limiting fast-food and heavily processed foods. Choose water or milk instead of sugary or energy drinks. Of course, sweet treats are definitely OK to enjoy, but it's all about moderation.

✓ If you notice yourself becoming overly preoccupied with eating, calories, weight, or your body size, please talk to your doctor, therapist, or someone else you trust.

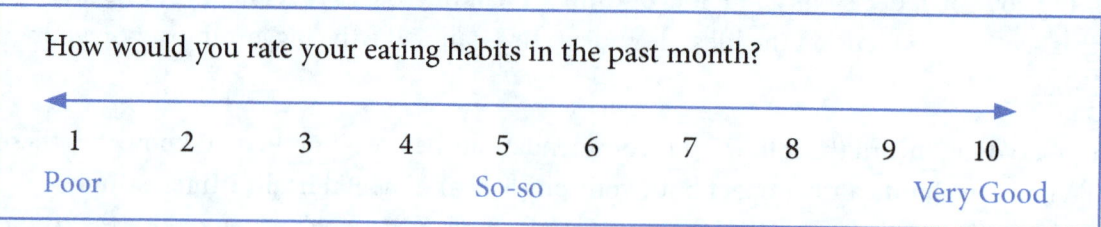

How would you rate your eating habits in the past month?

1   2   3   4   5   6   7   8   9   10
Poor   So-so   Very Good

Get Enough Sleep

✓ Strive for 8-10 hours of sleep per night.

✓ Keep a regular sleep schedule as much as possible.

✓ Avoid caffeine in the evening.

✓ Create a relaxing evening routine (bath, reading, journaling, calming music, etc.).

✓ Avoid screentime for 1 hour before bedtime.

✓ Try to avoid naps during the day.

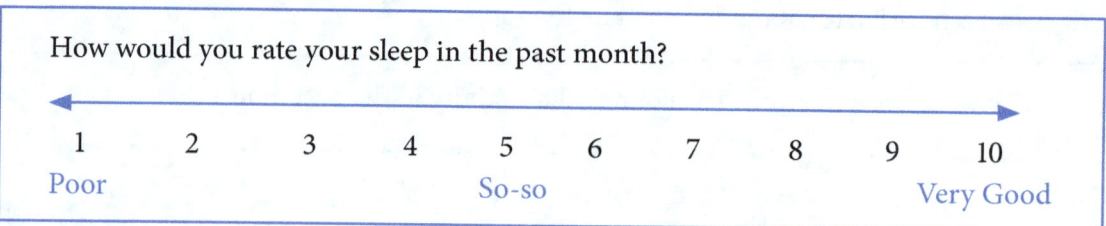

How would you rate your sleep in the past month?

1   2   3   4   5   6   7   8   9   10
Poor   So-so   Very Good

At the same time, it's important to consider the following three habits as well:

- Drinking alcohol

- Using drugs, including marijuana

- Smoking cigarettes / using nicotine

Many teenagers experiment with substances, and peer pressure to drink and use drugs can be intense. As discussed in Chapter 7, people often turn to alcohol and drugs to try to feel better, but some end up having more problems in the long run.

In this context, we want you to know that using substances may increase your risk for depression and other mental illnesses. Alcohol, drugs, and nicotine can also worsen psychological well-being and decrease the effectiveness of mental health medications. In addition, studies have shown that marijuana can affect normal brain development, increasing the risk of developing problems with memory, learning, and judgment. We recognize these substances are a huge part of our culture…. but there are risks that we want you to understand.

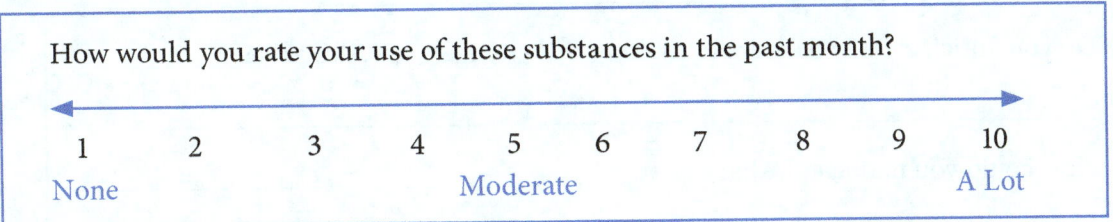

How would you rate your use of these substances in the past month?

1	2	3	4	5	6	7	8	9	10
None				Moderate					A Lot

Ready to Make a Change?

As you think through these lifestyle habits, perhaps something stands out to you. Are you ready to make a change? Writing down your plan can be a great way to kick-start the process. Remember that making a change is usually not a one-and-done deal. You may need to recommit and come back to it several times—which is perfectly OK.

Is there a behavior you want to work on? If so, which one?

Be physically active   Avoid or limit alcohol use   Other: _____

Eat a healthy diet   Avoid or limit drug use

Get enough sleep   Avoid or limit nicotine

What specifically will you do?_____

_____

What difference might that change make in your life?_____

_____

Is there someone who could support you in making this change? Perhaps help hold you accountable? If so, who? _____

_____

Do you anticipate any barriers to making this change? If so, describe: _____

_____

How could you manage the barrier(s)? _____

_____

If you're ready to start, when might you begin? _____

_____

5. Build Resilience to Cope With Challenges

As we discussed in Chapter 8, *resilience* refers to your ability to cope with difficult life situations. It's being able to face and deal with the inevitable challenges that come your way—and to bounce back and keep going. Fortunately, it's a skill that can be learned and improved over time.

The lifestyle habits from the preceding section are a great foundation for building resilience, and we have described many other useful skills throughout this book. Because this information is so important, we wanted to summarize all of these suggestions here. You might want to flag or tear out these pages as a reminder of specific things you can do today.

> I really think a champion is defined not by their wins but by how they can recover when they fall.
>
> Serena Williams

Relationships

- Reach out and stay connected to people you trust (pets count!)
- Help others, even in small ways
- Avoid isolating
- Ask for help when you need it

Activities and Schedule

- Make time to relax
- Remember to play
- Realize change is the one constant in life so try to be flexible
- Try to stick to a schedule or routine, especially when life feels chaotic
- Spend time in GREEN spaces—parks, gardens, mountains, trails—and BLUE spaces—near lakes, rivers, pools, beaches

Feelings

- Accept all of your feelings and try to avoid judging them as good/bad or right/wrong
- Find ways to express your emotions in ways that work for you and with safe people
- Use healthy coping tools
- Hold onto hope
- When you are hurting, treat yourself like you would a good friend

Mindset

- Remember your inner strength: You've gotten through hard times before and you can cope with this now
- Look for meaning in challenges: Ask yourself, "What can I learn from this?"
- Focus on what you have control over
- Tackle problems head on rather than ignoring or avoiding them
- Choose optimism, and surround yourself with people who share that mindset

Lifestyle Choices

- Be physically active on a regular basis (don't forget strength training)
- Eat a healthy diet
- Get enough sleep
- Minimize or monitor your use of substances including alcohol, drugs, and nicotine

Just as it takes commitment and effort to be physically strong, it takes practice to build and maintain your resilience as well. None of the strategies discussed in this chapter are guarantees, nor can they completely eliminate the possibility of your developing a mental illness. However, these skills may lower your risk, and they can help you cope effectively if a mental illness does emerge.

If you are currently experiencing emotional problems or if you develop a mental illness in the future, remember you are definitely not alone. Many effective treatments exist, and recovery is possible! We hope the information and tools provided in this book are useful in your journey, and we encourage you to seek professional help. Learning about mental illness, being aware of warning signs, getting help early, making healthy lifestyle choices, and building your resilience are solid tools that can help you with whatever comes your way.

CHAPTER 17

Lessons Learned

Before wrapping up, we invite you to take a few minutes to reflect on the lessons you have learned in your family's experience with mental illness.

Chapter 8 talked about ways in which your parent may have grown and gotten stronger as they manage mental illness or past trauma. Family members can also grow as they walk through difficult times in their family. Take a minute to think about this....

What Have You Learned About Yourself?

For example, some teens learn that:

- I am pretty strong and can handle a lot.

- Though all of this, I've become a better listener.

- Even when my parent is having a rough time, I need to keep up with my friends and activities. It's OK to set limits and take care of myself.

- Although my inner critic can be intense and I can get pretty down, I have learned how to be kind to myself—which makes a big difference.

- I have a lot of people who care about me.

- Even when my feelings seem out of control, I know I will be OK. There are things I can do to feel better.

> *By supporting my parent, "I consider myself a better person: more empathetic, more open to the problems of others."*
> **Daniel**[3]

- It's easy for me to over-think and anticipate the worst when I'm scared. I've learned I can catch myself when that happens and prevent my anxiety from spiraling. I usually either distract myself or talk to my best friend.

- Even though I can't fix the problems in my family, I can accept the reality of the situation. I support my parents and siblings the best I can.

How about you?

I have learned _____

_____

_____

_____

_____

_____

What Have You Learned About Your Family?

For example, some young people learn that:

- My family comes together when things are stressful.

- I appreciate how my aunt and grandpa step in to help when my mom is having a hard time.

- Some relatives will never really understand or support my dad. That stinks but we've given up trying to change them. It's better to move on and appreciate the many friends and family members who do show up for us.

- I am thankful for the fun times I have with my family.

- My stepmom may deal with her mental illness the rest of her life. Our family works hard to enjoy the good times, and we do our best to support her when she's struggling.

- My family really isn't that different from my friends' families. Although we are dealing with mental illness, everyone has problems.

How about you?

I have learned _____

_____

_____

_____

_____

_____

Thank you for dedicating your time and energy to working through this book. We hope that the concepts and skills you have learned are helpful.

In the future you may want to come back and refresh your memory on key facts, respond to some of the reflection questions, or find specific resources. Your family's journey with mental illness will undoubtedly shift over time, so the sections of this book that resonate with you may change as well.

Just as we encouraged you to offer your parent grace, we hope you give yourself the same kindness and compassion as you navigate this challenging situation. We encourage you to hold onto hope, focus on what you can control, and remember that you are never alone.

List of Feelings

afraid	crabby	furious	left out	sad
alone	criticized	guilty	lonely	safe
angry	curious	happy	lost	scared
annoyed	depressed	helpless	loved	strong
anxious	disappointed	hopeful	mad	surprised
ashamed	discouraged	hopeless	numb	suspicious
bored	disgusted	hurt	overwhelmed	tense
calm	disrespected	impatient	panicky	thankful
cheerful	embarrassed	insecure	powerless	unappreciated
compassionate	empty	invisible	protective	upset
confident	forgotten	jealous	proud	worried
confused	frustrated	judged	resentful	

Activities to Help Get Through the Rough Times

Bake cookies

Board games

Bowling

Clean or organize something

Color in coloring books

Cook, perhaps a new recipe

Create a playlist of favorite songs

Dance

Do a crossword puzzle

Doodle or draw

Eat a snack

Enjoy a walk or run

Fish

Get a manicure or pedicure

Go shopping

Go to the beach

Go to a coffee shop

Hang out with friends

Hike a nature trail

Hit the gym

Ice skate

Journal

Lift weights

Listen to music or a podcast

Make jewelry

Mini golf

Paint

Perform a random act of kindness

Plant a garden

Play a musical instrument

Play with siblings

Play with pets

Pray or meditate

Read a book or magazine

Ride a bike

Sidewalk chalk

Square breathing

Swim

Take a bath or shower

Take a nap

Text or talk to your friends

Think about 3 things you're grateful for

Try a relaxation app

Video games

Visit a museum

Volunteer

Wash the car

Watch TV, videos, or a movie

Work on your car

Write or read poetry

Yoga

Other(s): _____

RESOURCE LIST

Trustworthy Organizations

These websites have facts about mental illness, trauma, and substance use disorders. Organizations that offer classes and peer-support programs are indicated with an asterisk.*

National Alliance on Mental Illness (NAMI)* . . . . www.nami.org

Depression & Bipolar Support Alliance (DBSA)* . . . . www.dbsalliance.org

Anxiety and Depression Association of America * . . . . www.adaa.org

Mental Health America . . . . www.mhanational.org

National Center for PTSD . . . . www.ptsd.va.gov

Alcoholics Anonymous * . . . . www.aa.org

Al-Anon and Alateen Family Groups * . . . . www.al-anon.org

International Organizations Supporting Youth Whose Parent Has a Mental Illness

Children of Parents With a Mental Illness (COPMI),
Emerging Minds, Australia (information and videos for
youth whose parent has a mental illness) . . . . www.copmi.net.au

Our Time: For Children of Parents With a Mental Illness,
United Kingdom (videos, workshops, information, and
school-based programs) . . . . www.ourtime.org.uk

Books

At the time of writing, we are unaware of other current, reputable nonfiction books for teens about parental mental illness. The following books are written for adults who love someone managing mental illness.

General

Family intervention guide to mental illness: Recognizing symptoms and getting treatment. (2007). B. Morey & K. Mueser. New Harbinger.

I am not sick, I don't need help! How to help someone accept treatment. (2020). X. Amador. Vida Press.

Loving someone with a mental illness or history of trauma: Skills, hope, and strength for your journey. (2025). M. D. Sherman & D. M. Sherman. Johns Hopkins University Press.

When someone you love has a mental illness: A handbook for family, friends, and caregivers. (2003). R. Woolis. Penguin Group.

You are not alone: The NAMI guide to navigating mental health. (2022). K. Duckworth. Zando.

Bipolar Disorder

Bipolar disorder: A guide for you and your loved one. (2020). F. M. Mondimore. Johns Hopkins University Press.

The bipolar disorder survival guide: What you and your family need to know (3rd ed.). (2019). D. J. Miklowitz. Guilford.

Depression

Helping others with depression: Words to say, things to do. (2020). S. Noonan. Johns Hopkins University Press.

When someone you love is depressed: How to help your loved one without losing yourself. (1997). L. Rosen & X. Amador. Fireside.

PTSD

Loving someone with PTSD: A practical guide to understanding and connecting with your partner after trauma. (2014). A. Matsakis. New Harbinger.

The body keeps the score: Brain, mind, and body in the healing of trauma. (2015). B. van der Kolk. Penguin.

Trauma and recovery. (2022). J. Herman. Basic Books.

Schizophrenia

Surviving schizophrenia: A manual for families, patients and providers (7th ed). (2019). E. F. Torrey. Harper Perennial.

The complete family guide to schizophrenia: Helping your loved one get the most out of life. (2006). K. T. Mueser & S. Gingerich. Guilford.

Hotlines

911

24/7 service for medical emergencies. Call or text.

988: Suicide & Crisis Lifeline

24/7 free, confidential services if wanting emotional support for yourself or if you're worried about someone you love. Call, text, or chat via website 988lifeline.org

Trevor Project

24/7 free service for LGBTQ youth desiring support, including thinking about suicide, feeling lonely, or wanting someone to talk to. Call 866-488-7386 or text START to 678-678 or chat via website www.thetrevorproject.org

YouthLine

Free, confidential peer support line where teens can talk to other young people about any concern that bothers them—it can be a crisis or more general support. Answered daily by teens 4pm-10pm PST. Run by Lines for Life. Call 877-968-8491 or text "TEEN2TEEN" to 839863 or chat via website www.theyouthline.org

NOTE FOR PARENTS AND CAREGIVERS

Having a parent with a mental illness can be a challenging journey. Oftentimes young people grapple with questions, such as:

- How can I cope when my parent is struggling?

- What do I tell my friends?

- Will I develop mental health problems?

- How can I help my parent?

Teenagers can react to their parent's illness in a variety of ways. Some youth grow up quickly and take on extra responsibilities around the house, such as caring for younger siblings. While these kids may appear mature and confident, inside they can feel alone and scared. Other teens "act out" due to their anger about what is happening at home. Young people may blame themselves for their parent's struggles, which can stir up feelings of confusion and guilt. Oftentimes parents and other relatives are busy helping the person with the illness, so teens' feelings may be unintentionally overlooked.

This book deals directly with the teenager's experience and is organized in four sections:

Part One, **"Getting Started,"** introduces the book, including eight key facts that are explored in later chapters. We also invite the reader to do a mini self-assessment of how things are going for them and their family.

Part Two, **"Understanding the Basics,"** covers important issues about mental illness and trauma, including common symptoms, causes, co-occurring addictions, and treatment options. Accurate information is critical to living well with mental illness in the family.

Part Three, **"Living With a Parent Who Has a Mental Illness or History of Trauma,"** provides opportunities for readers to explore their feelings and learn research-based coping skills. This section normalizes a variety of emotional reactions and encourages the reader to write about their thoughts and feelings. Challenges related to dealing with stigma around mental illness and talking with friends are also explored, and tips are offered for handling crisis situations.

Part Four, **"Taking Care of Your Own Mental Health,"** helps readers understand and manage their own risk for developing a mental illness. Teens are encouraged to focus on what they can control, and are taught specific strategies to build their resilience.

Many reflection questions are sprinkled throughout the book, and we encourage readers to seek out additional information. Your teen may come to you wanting advice and support. If that happens, try to be open to their thoughts and feelings. As ongoing communication is key for families managing any difficult situation, thank them for coming to you. If you are unable to provide support at the time, assure your child that you love them and help them find someone to talk to, possibly a therapist, family member, spiritual leader, or teacher.

It's important that your child feels comfortable writing about their feelings in this book. Determine in advance if it's a private diary that no one else will read or if they want to use the journal sections as a way of starting a dialogue with you. Either approach is OK—please just clarify at the beginning.

We hope this book stimulates discussion in your family, and that it can be a helpful tool to educate, support, and empower your child.

NOTE FOR PROFESSIONALS

More than half of all people worldwide experience a mental illness at some point during their lifetime. Approximately 18% of children live with a parent who has a mental illness, and 4-7% live with a parent with a serious mental illness. These kids often experience a wide range of feelings—sadness, anxiety, embarrassment, confusion, anger, and guilt. Research has also found these young people to be at increased risk for many short- and long-term emotional, behavioral, and physical health problems.

In writing the second edition of this book, we realize that a lot has changed for teenagers in the past ~20 years. Young people now have access to information in ways that were previously unthinkable. They are exposed to seemingly incessant trauma on the news, and they live in a time of challenging societal issues such as global pandemics, racism, gun violence, cyberbullying, climate change, and the significant growth of loneliness. A lot has also happened in the realm of mental illness, including the development of promising therapies and medications and the infusion of recovery principles in care. Sadly, however, rates of mental illness have increased, and many people are unable to access the care they need.

Unfortunately, minimal progress has been made in the healthcare arena with respect to identifying and supporting the millions of offspring of parents with a mental illness. Most providers do not consistently inquire about or connect these youth with resources, which contributes to kids being unseen and feeling alone. The mental health care system continues to be quite fragmented and siloed, with adult and youth mental health professionals often not able to collaborate. The past two decades have not witnessed significant, widespread growth in prevention or clinical initiatives for these young people in the United States. [Kudos to the noteworthy international efforts listed in the Resource List, such as the United Kingdom-based OurTime program. They offer workshops for youth whose parent has a mental illness and educational curricula that classroom teachers can implement to open conversation and raise awareness about mental health and illness.]

This updated and expanded second edition is grounded in our desire to help fill the gap in available resources for teens. We offer facts based on the latest research, practical tips, actionable coping strategies, and stories from youth with lived experience of parental mental illness. Specifically, we strive to:

- ✓ Normalize teens' feelings and experience

- ✓ Educate youth about mental illness and trauma

- ✓ Encourage teens to use healthy coping strategies

- ✓ Teach teens strategies for managing their own risk for emotional problems and bolstering their resilience

- ✓ Empower youth in navigating stigma and how to talk with friends

- ✓ Provide teens tools to strengthen their relationship with their parent

- ✓ Offer resources for further learning

This hopeful yet honest book can be useful for anyone working with teenagers and families—mental health professionals, peer support specialists, clergy, teachers, family physicians, and pediatricians. Field testing has shown that the book is well suited for youth ages 11–18. However, it can be adapted to other age groups. As documented in the research on the health benefits of writing about emotional issues, we anticipate readers will benefit from the reflection activities scattered throughout the book.

As a psychologist/teacher, daughter/mother co-author team, we are fervent in our mission of helping these young people know they are not alone, arming them with knowledge and skills, and supporting entire families in opening the door to conversations about mental illness and trauma. We hope this is a useful resource as you support young people and their families.

ACKNOWLEDGMENTS

Our sincere and heartfelt thank you to the many people—adults and youth—who generously shared their time to review our book. Your support and insightful input helped us tremendously along this journey. The creation of this book and its second edition was truly a community effort.

A few families allowed us the privilege of entering into their lives and hearing their stories. What you gave us cannot be measured. We will forever be grateful for your honesty and vulnerability.

Many thanks to Jeff Zuckerman, MA MSW, our editor, who not only ensured that we followed writing style guidelines, but also provided invaluable content suggestions (consistently with a great sense of humor).

Special gratitude for our amazing graphic designer, James Monroe Design, for creating our beautiful website as well as the cover and interior design of this second edition.

Shout out to Luke (nephew/grandson) for his amazing work as a social media and marketing consultant. Thank you for helping us get our message out in a thoughtful, engaging way. So grateful!

Thanks to Lisa (sister/daughter) for your consistent encouragement, creativity, feedback, editing, and willingness to help with any request we made. Lisa, we know that we can always count on you for support, and we really thank you!

We want to say a special thank you to Dudley (dad/husband) for truly joining us in our book-writing journey. We cannot even begin to list the numerous contributions you make to this process, but it includes some difficult matters such as finances, taxes, and record keeping. Your support of this journey is invaluable. Thanks, Dad/Dud!

REFERENCES

1. Radmacher, M. A. (2019). *Courage doesn't always roar.* Conari Press.

2. National Association of Peer Supporters. (2021). *National practice guidelines for peer supporters.* https://www.peersupportworks.org/wp-content/uploads/2021/02/nationalguidelines_updated.pdf

3. Villatte, A., Piché, G., & Habib, R. (2020). *When your parent has a mental illness: Tips and testimonies from young people.* Université du Québec en Outaouais: Lapproche Laboratory.

4. National Association for Children of Alcoholics. (2011). *Kit for early childhood professionals.* https://nacoa.org

5. Nouwen, H. J. M. (1990). *The road to daybreak: A spiritual journey.* Image Press.

6. Obama, M. (2017, February 16). *Let's change the conversation around mental health.* www.huffingtonpost.co.uk/michelle-obama/lets-change-the-conversation-around-mental-health_b_9245816.html

7. Covey, S. R. (2001). *The 7 habits of highly effective people: Powerful lessons in personal change.* Free Press.

ABOUT THE AUTHORS

Michelle D. Sherman, PhD LP ABPP (she/her) is a licensed clinical psychologist who has dedicated her career to supporting families dealing with a mental illness or trauma/PTSD. She has worked in diverse settings, including the Veterans Affairs (VA) healthcare system, private practice, and academia as a Professor at the University of Oklahoma and University of Minnesota Medical Schools.

Dr. Sherman is a Fellow of the American Psychological Association (APA), and is Board Certified in Couple and Family Psychology. She is the Editor in Chief of *Couple and Family Psychology: Research and Practice,* the journal of APA's Society of Couple and Family Psychology, and was named their Family Psychologist of the Year in 2022. She has published over 75 articles in peer-reviewed journals, and has given several hundred workshops nationally and internationally. She served on the Board of the Oklahoma National Alliance on Mental Illness (NAMI) for 14 years and now enjoys volunteering with the Minnesota NAMI affiliate.

DeAnne M. Sherman (she/her), Michelle's mother, is a mental health advocate, French teacher, and choreographer. She graduated from St. Catherine University in St. Paul, Minnesota, where she received degrees in French, education, and speech/theater. She volunteers with NAMI-Minnesota, gives workshops with her daughter about mental illness in the family, and mentors people of all ages in the performing arts. DeAnne's mission is to affirm, educate, and empower others; she has strong passions for combating stigma, offering hope to people who are hurting, celebrating diversity, and promoting open discussion about mental health.

The collaboration of psychologist and teacher, daughter and mother, brings true synergy to Michelle and DeAnne's writing. The Shermans draw from their professional and personal life experiences which are the inspiration and foundation for their work.